GOD'S ONGOING GIFTS TO THE CHURCH

Nilson Leal de Sá, C.B.

GOD'S
ONGOING GIFTS
TO THE CHURCH

*Issues Confronting Ecclesial Movements
and New Communities*

SOPHIA INSTITUTE PRESS
Manchester, New Hampshire

Cover by Updatefordesign Studio

Cover image: *Priests Processing through Congregation*
courtesy of Community of the Beatitudes

Excerpts from the English translation of the *Catechism of the Catholic Church* for use
in the United States of America copyright © 1994, United States Catholic Conference, Inc.—Libreria Editrice Vaticana. English translation of the *Catechism of the
Catholic Church: Modifications from the Editio Typica* copyright © 1997, United
States Conference of Catholic Bishops, Inc.—Libreria Editrice Vaticana.

Nihil Obstat
Rev. Thomas J. Scherer, J.C.L.
Censor Librorum

Imprimatur
+Most Reverend Samuel J. Aquila, S.T.L.
Archbishop of Denver
Denver, Colorado, USA
February 7, 2023

Cum Permissu
Sr. Anna Katharina Pollmeyer, C.B.
President of the Community of the Beatitudes
Blagnac, France
January 30, 2023

Sophia Institute Press
Box 5284, Manchester, NH 03108
1-800-888-9344
www.SophiaInstitute.com

Sophia Institute Press is a registered trademark of Sophia Institute.

paperback ISBN 979-8-88911-064-4

ebook ISBN 979-8-88911-065-1

Library of Congress Control Number: 2023943222

Contents

CHAPTER I
Charism

CHAPTER II
The Founders

CHAPTER III
Institutionalization of the Charism

CHAPTER IV
STATES OF LIFE

CHAPTER V
CONSECRATION

CHAPTER VI
COMMUNITY LIFE

CHAPTER VII
THE FORMATION

CHAPTER VIII
LITURGY

CHAPTER IX
RELATION TO THE LOCAL CHURCH

CHAPTER X
"ECCLESIAL FAMILIES"

PREFACE

THE HOLY SPIRIT ALWAYS accompanies the Church's mission, enriching it with His gifts. Among these, recent Popes have taught that ecclesial movements and new communities are providential gifts of the Spirit of God and signs of His fruitfulness. Furthermore, "the entire Church, as beloved Pope John Paul II used to say, is one great movement animated by the Holy Spirit, a river that travels through history to irrigate it with God's grace and make it full of life, goodness, beauty, justice and peace" (Benedict XVI, *Regina Caeli* [June 4, 2006]).

The Second Vatican Council clearly reaffirms the equality and common dignity among the baptized, expressed both in the faithful's participation in the same ecclesial mission and in the common vocation to holiness and the perfection of charity. The new associations are places of evangelical life — where a charism is shared by people of different living conditions — and they are rich with the conciliar doctrine on the People of God and communion. Furthermore, in their own way, they express Christian brotherhood in charity.

Certainly, God's action today—particularly after the Second Vatican Council, which contributed greatly to the emergence and maturation of these realities—is an effective response to the challenges of our time. Consequently, these gifts are necessary for the life of the Church, for her mission and for her building up in unity, thanks to the apostolic ministry of the bishops in communion with the Successor of Peter. Pastors and the entire People of God ought to be receptive to these gifts, despite the difficulties. Within this context, this work offers opportune pastoral and canonical reflections on ecclesial movements and new communities.

These ecclesial realities enrich the experience of charity in communion and are powerful expressions of brotherhood. In them we perceive the harmony and complementarity of the different vocations, charisms, and ministries that lead to the fraternal building of the Body of Christ, according to the Father's will and under the guidance of the Holy Spirit. In this way ecclesial movements and new communities can be a force for consolidating brotherhood among peoples and a healthy challenge to authentic evangelical witness.

In fact, in this secularized and individualistic world, movements and communities awaken in the faithful the awareness of belonging to the Church. Indeed, its vitality is accompanied by a great missionary dynamism. In this way, collaboration between new associative realities and older structures proves to be very fruitful for the evangelization of social and cultural life. New ecclesial realities can also positively influence parish renewal.

In addition, these movements and communities offer the faithful an opportunity to receive adequate formation, rediscovering, in particular, the sacraments of Christian initiation. For this reason, the presence of these new associations contributes significantly to the maturing of Christian life: families find a valid support that reinforces the grace of Catholic marriage and young people are encouraged to fully develop their baptismal vocation.

Reading this work, we realize the challenges that new associations face. At the same time, this book offers clear elements that deserve attention, especially given the author's experiences in Africa, the Americas, Asia, and Europe. This work will also be useful to pastors navigating discernment. Likewise, members of ecclesial movements and new communities, as well as those interested in this topic, will benefit greatly. Thus, encouraged to share and serve the unique mission of the Church, everyone will feel motivated to transmit with enthusiasm "the joy of the Gospel" (Pope Francis).

Cardinal Manuel Monteiro de Castro
Emeritus Major Penitentiary of the Apostolic Penitentiary

GOD'S ONGOING GIFTS TO THE CHURCH

INTRODUCTION

For years I have noticed the importance of offering reflections on new communities and other new ecclesial realities. Today there is already good international documentation, which clarifies this rich and flourishing novelty.

My purpose, however, is to go deeper, while not exhausting a subject full of vitality and surprises. Living thirty years in a new community, which went through an international expansion but also its moments of serious internal crises, as well as my time in Africa, the Americas, and Europe, gives me a certain vision of this field's international scope.

Above all, I am coming from a pastoral perspective, without failing to highlight some theological and canonical aspects. And when reflecting on these new communities, there are several gateways that are not exclusive: canonical, theological, sociological, or others. The complementarity of disciplines can only enrich the topic dealt with. I hope this modest work will contribute to increased associations along with the institutionalization of each charism, thus advancing the Holy Spirit's fruitful mission in the heart of the Church.

CHAPTER I

CHARISM

God's Gift

ACCORDING TO ST. PAUL, a charism is a gift from God for the edification of the Church (see 1 Cor. 12; Rom. 12:6–8). The *Catechism of the Catholic Church* (no. 799) also states:

> Whether extraordinary or simple and humble, charisms are graces of the Holy Spirit which directly or indirectly benefit the Church, ordered as they are to her building up, to the good of men, and to the needs of the world.

In consecrated life, charism has often been identified with the specific purpose of the institute, with its apostolate, or sometimes used to designate the more interior or spiritual aspect of an institute of consecrated life, almost in opposition to the institutional dimension.

When the Second Vatican Council deals with the theme of consecrated life and its institutes it never speaks of charism. [1] Instead, it uses such words as: primitive spirit or spirit of the

---

[1] In fact, one speaks of the religious, according to the terminology in use at that time. The new *Code of Canon Law* uses *consecrated life*, including in this generic notion religious, members of secular institutes, as well as consecrated virgins, hermits, and new forms of consecrated life.

founders, own particular characteristics and work, sound traditions, patrimony, the manner of living, praying, and working.[2]

The *Code of Canon Law* does not use the term *charism* either,[3] but a terminology similar to that of the Council: the mind of the founders, that is, their designs and purposes, the nature of the institute, as well as its spirit and own character, its sound traditions, all of which constitute its charismatic patrimony (see canons 578; 598 §1).[4]

It can be said, therefore, that the "Charism of the Founders" is an "*experience of the Spirit*, transmitted to their disciples to be lived, safeguarded, deepened and constantly developed by them, in harmony with the Body of Christ continually in the process of growth." This charism "also involves a particular style of sanctification and of apostolate, which creates its particular tradition,"[5]

---

[2] See Second Vatican Council, Dogmatic Constitution *Lumen gentium* on the Church (November 21, 1964), no. 45a; Decree *Perfectae caritatis* on the Adaptation and Renewal of Religious Life (October 28, 1965), nos. 2b; 3a.

[3] In the 1977 schema of the *Code*, *charism* was found in several canons.

[4] Indeed "the charismatic patrimony, originating in the person of the founder, is shared in and deepened, thereby giving life to true spiritual families. The new ecclesial groups, in their diverse forms present themselves as shared charismatic gifts. Ecclesial movements and new communities show how a determinate founding charism can gather the faithful together and help them to live fully their Christian vocation and proper state of life in service of the ecclesial mission." Dicastery for the Doctrine of the Faith, Letter *Iuvenescit Ecclesia* to the Bishops of the Catholic Church Regarding the Relationship between Hierarchical and Charismatic Gifts in the Life and the Mission of the Church (May 15, 2016), no. 16.

[5] Dicastery for Bishops, Directives *Mutuae relationes* for the Mutual Relations between Bishops and Religious in the Church (May 14, 1978), no. 11.

becoming a "foundation charism."[6] Charism, therefore, is a spiritual heritage that communicates itself.

When talking about the charism or spiritual heritage of an institution, one must understand both the founders' general intuition or inspiration ("experience of the Spirit") as well as the project, that is, the means for the general intuition's realization ("peculiar style of sanctification and apostolate"). In this way, not only is the divine origin of the gift made through its founders affirmed, but its historical content is also expressed, as it is concretely manifested, emphasizing an aspect of the life of Christ or of the mystery of the Church.[7]

The Magisterium does not define a new community's charism, nor is it necessary. In fact, based on what has been said above and by analogy, it is possible to understand an association of the

---

[6] See Marta Balog, "Charisme fondateur," *Studia canonica* 50 (2016): 165–174.

[7] For example, an institute that claims to have a contemplative charism highlights the peculiar attitude of Jesus who withdrew alone to pray. Another, dedicated to health, shows the closeness of the Lord to the sick. Also, the one who works in education manifests the attention of Christ who instructed His disciples in virtue. An association that speaks of the charism of "communion" reflects a dimension of the mystery of the Church. "Each one expresses, according to the charism, certain aspects of the ineffable mystery of Christ and of the Church, without pretending to exhaust its richness or the totality of the gifts of the spirit." National Conference of Bishops of Brazil (CNBB), *Igreja particular, movimentos eclesiais e novas comunidades—Particular church, ecclesial movements and new communities* (Brasília: Edições CNBB, 2009), 41.

Highlighting an aspect of Christ's life or the Church's, an institute's charism calls all the baptized to important dimensions of the common mission: intimacy with God in prayer is a call for all the faithful (not only for Carmelites); to help the sick and the poor befits everyone (not exclusively the Franciscans); transmitting the Good News is everyone's duty (not a Dominican prerogative); building communion in the diversity of gifts is a task for all Christians (not a privilege for new associations).

faithful's charism, which, like an institute of consecrated life, gathers disciples around its founders. The charism encompasses a community's rich heritage: its character and physiognomy, its traditions, its way of being, of praying, of carrying out its apostolates. Indeed, a charism has its own spirit and purpose.

In ecclesial movements and new communities, "the original charism ... is a particular gift of the Holy Spirit that gives rise to a concrete fraternity and whose *raison d'être* coincides in fact with the apostolic purpose of the Church." This founders' charism is "constantly characterized by a strong experience of *communio fidelium* [communion of the faithful], as a concrete reality of the family."[8]

Mutuae relationes, no. 12 also offers a timely and encouraging observation:

> Every authentic charism implies a certain element of genuine originality and of special initiative for the spiritual life of the Church. In its surroundings it may appear troublesome and may even cause difficulties, since it is not always and immediately easy to recognize it as coming from the Spirit. The specific charismatic note of any institute demands, both of the Founder and of his disciples, a continual examination regarding fidelity to the Lord; docility to His Spirit; intelligent attention to circumstances and an outlook cautiously directed to the signs of the times; the will to be part of the Church; the awareness of subordination to the sacred hierarchy; boldness of initiatives; constancy in the giving of self; humility in bearing with adversities. The true relation between genuine charism, with its perspectives of newness, and interior suffering, carries with it an unvarying history of the connection between charism and cross, which, above every motive that may

---

[8]   Eugenio Corecco, *Ius et communio* (Casale Monferrato: Piemme, 1997), 239.

justify misunderstandings, is supremely helpful in discerning the authenticity of a vocation.[9]

Pope Benedict XVI said these new charisms, which "the Spirit is now bringing about in the Church, not least through the ecclesial movements and the new communities," and He acts "with a view to the one body and in the unity of the one body.... These gifts, which awaken in many people the desire for a deeper spiritual life, can benefit not only the lay faithful but the clergy as well."[10]

On November 22, 2014 during a meeting with representatives of ecclesial movements and new communities, Pope Francis spoke on the founding charism of these new realities:

> It is necessary to preserve the *freshness of your charism*, never lose that freshness, the freshness of your charism, always renewing the "first love" (cf. Rev 2:4). As time goes by, there is a greater temptation to become comfortable, to become hardened in set ways of doing things, which, while reassuring, are nonetheless sterile. There is the temptation to cage in the Holy Spirit: this is a temptation! However, "realities are more important

[9] In the same perspective, Pope Francis gives another criterion to discern the authenticity of a charism, namely, *communion*: "The Holy Spirit would appear to create disorder in the Church, since he brings the diversity of charisms and gifts; yet all this, by his working, is a great source of wealth, for the Holy Spirit is the Spirit of unity, which does not mean uniformity, but which leads everything back to harmony. In the Church, it is the Holy Spirit who creates harmony. One of the Fathers of the Church has an expression which I love: the Holy Spirit himself is harmony — '*Ipse harmonia est.*' He is indeed harmony. Only the Spirit can awaken diversity, plurality and multiplicity, while at the same time building unity. Here too, when we are the ones who try to create diversity and close ourselves up in what makes us different and other, we bring division." Francis, Homily of Pentecost for the Ecclesial Movements (May 19, 2013), no. 2.

[10] Benedict XVI, Letter Proclaiming a Year for Priests (June 16, 2009).

than ideas" (cf. *Evangelii Gaudium*, 231–233); even if a certain institutionalization of the charism is necessary for its survival, we ought not delude ourselves into thinking that external structures can guarantee the working of the Holy Spirit. The newness of your experiences does not consist in methods or forms, or the newness itself, all of which are important, but rather in your willingness to respond with renewed enthusiasm to the Lord's call. Such evangelical courage has allowed for the growth of your Movements and New Communities. If forms and methods become ends in themselves, they become ideological, removed from reality which is constantly developing; closed to the newness of the Spirit, such rigid forms and methods will eventually stifle the very charism which gave them life. We need always to return to the sources of our charism, and thus to rediscover the driving force needed to respond to challenges.... You are ... always on the way, always in movement, always open to God's surprises which are in harmony with the first call of the movement, namely the founding charism.[11]

Pope Francis returned to this theme in the autumn of 2021. To maintain the "freshness of the charism," the Holy Father recommended:

> As members of associations of the faithful ... you have a genuinely ecclesial mission. With devotion you endeavor to live out and make fruitful those charisms that the

---

[11] Francis, Address to Participants in the Third World Congress of Ecclesial Movements and New Communities (November 22, 2014), no. 1. The Holy Father recalls also: "The founding charism ... is what ... was passed on by the founders and the first generation and for which all of you are equally responsible. [This] spiritual patrimony [is] welcomed by all, lived and shared by all, understood by all and entrusted to all." Address to the Members of the Movement of Cursillos of Christianity in Italy (May 28, 2022) (my translation).

Holy Spirit, through your founders, granted to all the members of your groups, to the benefit of the Church.... For this reason, the charism to which we belong must be furthered more and more, and we must always reflect together in order to incarnate it in the new situations we live in. To do this, great docility is required of us, and great humility, in order to recognize our limitations and accept to change outdated ways of doing and thinking, or methods of the apostolate that are no longer effective, or forms of organization of internal life that have proved inadequate or even harmful.[12]

An ecclesial movement or new community that loses the sense of its primary vocation suffers "diseases that come from the weakening of the founding charism, which becomes lukewarm and loses its capacity for attraction."[13] For this reason these associations "have the duty to verify, in assemblies or chapters, the state of the foundational charism and make the necessary changes in their own legislation (which will then be approved by the respective Dicastery)."[14]

A charism must be a living reality for those who are called to follow it.[15] Indeed, "the charism is not preserved in a bottle of distilled water! Faithfulness to the charism does not mean 'to petrify it'—the devil is the one who 'petrifies,' do not forget! Faithfulness to the charism does not mean to write it on a parchment and frame it. [It] cannot be reduced to a museum of records, of decisions taken, of the rules of conduct. It certainly

---

[12] Francis, Address to the Participants in the Meeting of Moderators of Lay Associations, Ecclesial Movements, and New Communities (September 16, 2021), no. 2.

[13] Ibid., no. 3.

[14] Ibid., no. 8.

[15] Pope Francis recalls that a "charism ... is like water. If it does not flow, it becomes foul." Address to the Participants in the General Chapter of the Missionary Sons of the Immaculate Heart of Mary (Claretians) (September 9, 2021) (my translation).

entails faithfulness to tradition, but faithfulness to tradition ...
'is not to worship the ashes but to pass on the flame.'"[16]A good
sign of healthiness is a missionary zeal, that "is proof of a radical
experience of ever renewed fidelity to one's charism that surpasses any kind of weary or selfish withdrawal."[17]

[16]   Francis, Address to the Communion and Liberation Movement (March
      7, 2015).
[17]   Benedict XVI, Message to the Participants of the Second World Con-
      gress on Ecclesial Movements and New Communities (May 22, 2006).

CHAPTER II

THE FOUNDERS

INSTRUMENTS OF THE LORD[18]

———•———∿•╱———•———

THE HOLY SPIRIT'S GIFT of a charism to the Church frequently comes through intermediaries; it passes through a person: the founder or foundress.[19] Sometimes there is a group of

---

[18] This chapter is partially inspired by Henry Donneaud, "La Communauté des Béatitudes: De l'appel monastique au témoignage missionnaire," *Bulletin de littérature ecclésiastique* 116 (2015): 99–116. Another important reference: Velasio De Paolis, *La vita consacrata nella Chiesa* (Venice: Marcianum Press, 2010), in particular pages 204–220.

About the Community of the Beatitudes, to which I belong, Saint Paul Publications published the founder's book: Ephraim, *Rains of the Late Season: The Holy Spirit at the Birth of a New Community* (Middlegreen: Saint Paul, 1992).

[19] In the beginning of a new institute or association, the presence of the founder may be a factor of stability until a more solid institutionalization of the charism is realized. Pope Francis said, having in mind the government of these realities: "We need to distinguish, in ecclesial movements (and also in religious congregations), between those that are in the process of formation and those that have already acquired a certain organic and juridical stability.... All institutes—whether religious or lay movements—... in formation ... [need] a certain stability of the superiors during this phase. It is important to make this distinction in order to be able to move more freely in discernment." Francis, Address (September 16, 2021), no. 8.

founders—one of whom is called the founder while the others are called co-founders—called to initiate a project and carry it out in a precise context.

The origin of an association often involves several people rather than one person, and therefore, the spirit and projects that proceed from an association can be a collective inspiration. However, the founders are only mediators of the divine gift given to the Church: "Through the founders and initiators of your Movements and Communities you have glimpsed the Face of Christ shining with special brightness and set out on your way."[20] Since the Church is the recipient, the spirit and projects of the founders must be submitted to her and verified by her.

Thus a dialogue is established between the founders and the competent ecclesiastical authority to accept the gift of God. Indeed, the founders must be helped to interpret this gift through the mediation of ecclesiastical authority, authentically reading the work of the Spirit. In this way, the physiognomy of the community or movement is defined: the charismatic patrimony composed of those elements is recognized by ecclesiastical authority.

This precision is fundamental because only certain gifts are meant to be transmitted from the founder to the community. It is important to distinguish the personal charism of the founders and the founding charism: the charism of a founder draws together and organizes a community in order to live the founding charism. This last one must be recognized by ecclesiastical authority and is part of the charismatic patrimony of the community. Not everything that is part of the founders' personality will be communicated to the Church through the association.

And this heritage is not necessarily what the founder intended to do, but what the Church recognized and concluded from this

---

[20] Benedict XVI, Message (May 22, 2006).

intention. In this way, she guarantees the authenticity of a particular charism and the evangelical goodness of its actions.[21] The juridical or canonical institutionalization and formalization of a new entity is also at the service of the Holy Spirit and of the charism itself, safeguarding its organic development within the Church.

A founder must always be at the service of the charism. The approved charism, not the founders, must be the regulator of the entire community. Otherwise, there would be a risk of idolizing them, putting them in a place that does not belong to them. The charism is a dimension that transcends everyone, starting with the founders themselves. Of course, they will be esteemed, respected, and asked for as advisors, but not as the "owners" of the charism.

Much has been said about founders recently — of institutes of consecrated life, ecclesial movements and new communities. If in several the sanctity of life was perceived, others proved to be "false prophets":

> Marcial Maciel remains a mysterious figure. There is, on the one hand, a life that, as we now know, was out of moral bounds — an adventurous, wasted, twisted life. On the other hand, we see the dynamism and the strength with which he built up the congregation of Legionaries.... Many [young men] have been called by a false figure to what is, in the end, right after all. That

---

[21] The *Explanatory Note*, no. 14 of Dicastery for Laity, Family, and Life, General Decree *The Associations of the Faithful* (June 3, 2021) affirms in this sense that the presence of the founders in the government, in the beginning of a new entity, ensures "that the charism received by them might be appropriately received in the Church and be faithfully assimilated by members,... if the [Dicastery] considers this opportune for the development and stability of the [international] association or entity, and if a dispensation [for a particular case] corresponds to the clear will of the central governing body."

is the remarkable thing, the paradox, that a false prophet, so to speak, could still have a positive effect.[22]

The revelation of a founder's faults is a real ordeal for a community. Questions about the pertinence and viability of the work inevitably arise: How can a bad tree bear good fruit?

A founder is the instrument of the charism, not its master and main author. He progressively receives the fundamental elements of the charism: it is not received as a whole, at the conception of the community. The charism—inscribed in a precise ecclesial and social context—develops and matures progressively, through the founder's successive inspirations. Docility to these inspirations allows him and his community to be guided by providence. However, even though the founder receives the elements of the charism, the Church alone is able to authenticate it, define it, correct it, clarify it, explain it, and articulate it in the ecclesial body, thanks to the Holy Spirit's guidance.

We must also distinguish between the founder's more or less profound or deficient holiness and the objectivity of the charism. The founder receives it and transmits it to the Church. She then judges the charism itself for its ecclesial, spiritual, doctrinal, and missionary value. The founder's personal holiness does not limit the charism nor is it intrinsically linked to the charism in order to condition it. The founder's exemplary sanctity—however precious to the community—does not belong to the essence of the charism itself. One does not follow a founder, but Christ, through specific charismatic modalities discerned by the Church. From Christ comes the sanctifying fruitfulness of a community, not from its founder.

---

[22] Benedict XVI, *Light of the World: The Pope, the Church, and the Signs of the Times; A Conversation with Peter Seewald* (San Francisco: Ignatius Press, 2010), 38–39.

The large number of deficient founders in the second half of the twentieth century—although other cases have occurred in the history of the Church—can be seen as a call not to idolize the figure of the founder, as if the quality of the foundation formally depended on the holiness of the founder.[23] In this regard, one should not unduly manipulate Jesus' words: "A good tree cannot bear bad fruit, nor can a rotten tree bear good fruit. Every tree that does not bear good fruit will be cut down and thrown into the fire. So by their fruits you will know them" (Matt. 7:18–20). In this passage Jesus does not invite us to judge the fruit by virtue of the tree, but, on the contrary, to judge the quality of the tree in view of the fruit it produces. Jesus' words cannot be falsified: the fruits are judged for themselves.

To judge the intrinsic quality of a community, the Church scrutinizes first the proper and objective nature of its charism and then the quality of the fruits it produces, particularly in terms of holiness and apostolic fruitfulness.

Even if this holiness, as expected, does not mature into fruit in the founder's lifetime, the charism may still well blossom from a tree he helped to plant. Christ, the source of all holiness, was never prevented from acting in the Church, even through her ministers—though accredited—were perhaps not the most virtuous or the most holy.

[23] Pope Francis expressed himself about this: "It's curious, it's very curious. Many [religious congregations and associations] with a novelty that was great, ended up in very difficult situations: they have ended up under apostolic visitation, they have ended up with terrible sins, they have been placed under commission ... But there are many and not only are these great ones that we know, which are scandalous, ... but also small ones. ... Cases of abuse of various kinds ... have occurred in these realities and [we] always find their root in the abuse of power. This is the origin: the abuse of power. Not infrequently the Holy See, in recent years, has had to intervene, launching difficult processes of rehabilitation." Francis, Address (September 16, 2021), no. 3.

The Church, more than ever, must maternally carry out her role of discernment in a prudent, lucid, patient, and benevolent way. In this way she can receive the Holy Spirit's treasured gifts that are actualized through fragile, earthen vessels.

CHAPTER III

INSTITUTIONALIZATION OF THE CHARISM

THE NEW ASSOCIATIONS

IN THE HISTORY OF the Church there has always been a phenomenon of lay aggregation in different forms: third orders, confraternities, and different forms of sodalities.[24] But the Holy Spirit "[is multifaceted in his gifts].... He breathes where he wills. He does so unexpectedly,... in ways previously unheard of."[25] In particular, many varied associative forms[26] flourished or were encouraged after the Second Vatican Council, whether they now claim existing spiritualities or

[24] See Juan José Echeverría, "Los movimientos eclesiales en los albores del siglo XXI," *Revista Española de Derecho Canónico* 58 (2001): 578. For a brief historical description: Maria Casey, "Associations of Christ's Faithful: Possibilities for the Future," *Studia canonica* 41 (2007): 81–82.

[25] Benedict XVI, Letter (June 16, 2009).

[26] Undoubtedly, "the movements have an earlier origin [than the Second Vatican Council] (La Obra de Maria was born in 1943; Communion and Liberation, in 1954; The Neocatechumenal Way, in 1964);... the new communities emerged in the 1970s ... in the charismatic renewal movement." Echeverría, "Los movimientos eclesiales," 582 (my translation). See also Christoph Hegge, "I movimenti ecclesiali e la ricezione del Concilio Vaticano II," *Periodica de re canonica* 88 (1999): 501; Arturo Cattaneo, "Los movimientos eclesiales: cuestiones eclesiológicas y canónicas," *Ius Canonicum* 76 (1998): 573; Dominic LeRouzès, "Le droit canonique et les communautés nouvelles," *Studia canonica* 40 (2006): 398.

bring new charismatic elements:[27] Pope John Paul II spoke of "a new era of group endeavors of the lay faithful [through] a multiplicity of group forms: associations, groups, communities, movements [as] a new era of group endeavors of the lay faithful."[28]

These new associative forms "are the fruit of Vatican Council II, in as much as the Council made possible, if not their birth, at least their growth and maturation,"[29] thanks to the richness of the Magisterium.[30] They constitute "one of the most important innovations inspired by the Holy Spirit in the Church for the implementation of the Second Vatican Council."[31] They

[27] See Paul Josef Cordes, *Benedetto XVI ispira i nuovi movimenti e le realtà ecclesiali: Il punto della situazione teologico-pastorale* (Vatican City: Libreria Editrice Vaticana, 2012), 22.

[28] John Paul II, Apostolic Exhortation *Christifideles laici* on the Vocation and the Mission of the Lay Faithful in the Church and in the World (December 30, 1988), no. 29. Cardinal Stanislaw Rylko speaks about a "new associative moment." *Ecclesial Movements and New Communities: The Response of the Holy Spirit to Today's Challenge of Evangelization* (Address given in Bogotá, March 9, 2006).

[29] Guzmán Carriquiry, "The Ecclesial Movements in the Religious and Cultural Context of the Present Day," in *The Ecclesial Movements in the Pastoral Concern of the Bishops*, ed. Pontifical Council for the Laity (Vatican City: Pontificium Consilium pro Laicis, 2000), 50. In this same sense see Philippe Gonzalez and Paul Philibert, "Les communautés nouvelles: Une réception de Vatican II," *Lumen vitae* 62 (2007): 419; Hegge, "I movimenti ecclesiali," 502; Laurent Villemin, "L'éclosion des nouveaux mouvements: Une question à l'ecclésiologie," *Lumen vitae* 62 (2007): 368.

[30] In fact, "the texts of the Council favored the growth of these experiences and opened the door to new ones. This is explicit in the Dogmatic Constitution *LG* (ch. IV), in the *GS* (ch. 43) or in the *PO* (ch. 8) and, above all, in the decree *AA* on the lay apostolate." CNBB, *Igreja particular*, 15. The Council wanted to promote a new ecclesiological and pastoral dynamic: see Cattaneo, "Los movimientos eclesiales," 573. The post-conciliar Magisterium deals more extensively with the theme of these associations: see Echeverría, "Los movimientos eclesiales," 577; CNBB, *Igreja particular*, 15–17 which, in this regard, offer a synthesis of the Magisterium from Paul VI to John Paul II.

[31] Benedict XVI, Address to Bishops and Representatives of Ecclesial Movements and New Communities (May 17, 2008).

belong "to the living structure of the Church"[32] and are, for her, a richness.[33]

1. CANONICAL STATUS

1.1 GENERAL CONSIDERATIONS

Under the terminology of *new associations*[34] are grouped associations of believers with very varied expressions:[35] ecclesial movements and new communities.[36]

For some, the notion of *ecclesial movement*[37] is synonymous with different forms of communities[38] and even, in *sensu lato*,

[32] Benedict XVI, Message (May 22, 2006). See also, on the contribution of John Paul II in this regard, Paul Josef Cordes, *Benedetto XVI ispira i nuovi movimenti*, 30.

[33] See Francis, Apostolic Exhortation *Evangelii gaudium* on the Proclamation of the Gospel in Today's World (November 24, 2013), no. 29.

[34] This is an expression of John Paul II: see *Christifideles laici*, no. 31.

[35] On this topic, we studied forty-four associations of the faithful whose statutes were approved by the former Pontifical Council for the Laity.

[36] See *Iuvenescit Ecclesia*, no. 2. For a clarification on this terminology see Jean Beyer, "Motus ecclesiales," *Periodica de re morali, canonica, liturgica* 75 (1986): 613–637. Pope Francis makes little use of it: in *Evangelii gaudium*, no. 29 he speaks of "movements and forms of association." The Canadian Conference of Catholic Bishops calls such a group "a *movement*, an *association*, a *community*, or a *fraternity*." *New Ecclesial Movements and Associations* (September 5, 2006).

[37] See Echeverría, "Los movimientos eclesiales," which presents a good summary of the various distinctions made between movements and communities, particularly on pages 582–585. For other types of movements see Silvia Recchi, "Per una configurazione canonica dei movimenti ecclesiali," *Quaderni di diritto ecclesiale* 11 (1998): 58–59; Marcelo Colombo, "Los nuevos movimientos eclesiales y su encuadramiento canónico en la Iglesia particular," *Anuario Argentino de Derecho Canónico* 14 (2007): 91–99.

[38] In fact, for some, "the notion of movement applies to communities that are different from each other, in their charisms, in their pedagogies, in their community forms, in their styles of diakonia." João Evangelista Martins Terra, *Os novos movimentos eclesiais* (São Paulo: Editora Canção Nova, 2010), 44.

includes not only the so-called new communities but also associations that regroup more massively.[39] From a linguistic point of view, "the term 'movement' does not have a single well-defined sense."[40]

New communities integrate a variety of shared charisms: prayer groups where members commit to a life of prayer, charity, evangelization, etc.; covenant or non-residential communities that, in addition, offer their members continuous formation and demand a commitment to their works; living or residential communities, whose members often take on the spirit of the evangelical counsels:[41]

> It would be presumptuous to offer a definition, since such a designation is used to qualify very different realities. Does the adjective *new* only refer to the fact that the community so designated is recent? But this expression seems to apply as much to communities born after Vatican II as to others that appeared much earlier. Or does one want to indicate the novelty of the proposed evangelical community's way of life? No doubt about it, but there is still a lot of variety here. Are these communities born in the Charismatic Renewal movement? This is the

---

[39] Some say that the notion of "movements" also includes "new communities." See Camillo Ruini, "Tangible Ecclesial Communion," in *Pastors and the Ecclesial Movements*, ed. Pontifical Council for the Laity (Vatican City: Libreria Editrice Vaticana, 2009), 197. M. Dortel-Claudot gives a quantitative criterion that seems relevant: *Les communautés nouvelles* (Paris: CEF, 1991), 4.

[40] Stanislaw Rylko, "The Event of 30 May 1998 and its Ecclesiological and Pastoral Consequences for the Life of the Church," in *The Ecclesial Movements in the Pastoral Concern of the Bishops*, ed. Pontifical Council for the Laity (Vatican City: Pontificium Consilium pro Laicis, 2000), 28. The fact is that "there is no definition of this ecclesial associative phenomenon by the legislator or accepted by the various authors." Echeverría, "Los movimientos eclesiales," 581.

[41] For this distinction see Echeverría, "Los movimientos eclesiales," 583. A similar typology of the new communities can be found in: Comité canonique français des religieux, *Vie religieuse, érémitisme, consécration des vierges, communautés nouvelles* (Paris: Cerf, 1993), 217–222.

case for many, but not all. The issue is as complex as the reality is rich, the notion of new community is an encompassing concept of diverse realities.[42]

After a new association is approved by the competent authority, the 1983 *Code of Canon Law* regulates it. Specifically, canons 298–329, under title V on *Associations of the Christian Faithful*, from the first part on *The Christian Faithful*, in book II on *The People of God*, govern the association.[43]

1.2 THE PRODUCTION OF THE STATUTES

This regulation contains fundamental elements. Namely, the membership of a movement or a new community implies rights and duties regarding formation (Christian but also specific to the charism), as well as participation in the apostolic action and mission of the entity. As the latter often has members from different states of life, the canonical condition of its members (lay single or married, ordained, consecrated) must be respected and protected (especially the rights and duties of family relationships, if the association admits them). These must be defined and detailed in the statutory norms of each association (see canon 304 §1):

[42] Tony Anatrella, *Développer la vie communautaire dans l'Église: L'exemple des Communautés nouvelles* (Dijon: Echelle Jacob, 2014), 13 (my translation).

Note for the English version: The first edition of this book was published before recent revelations about the conduct of Msgr. Tony Anatrella, one of the sources whose works are cited in this book. While these revelations are distressing and his actions must be condemned, his theological contributions to the Church cannot be dismissed easily and must be evaluated on their own merit. Aware of this, I have still included some of his writings in this newly translated edition because I have found them to be particularly incisive and illuminating on the present topic.

[43] These canons could include a great diversity of associations "avoiding juridical straitjackets that deaden the novelty which is born from the specific experience." *Iuvenescit Ecclesia*, no. 23.

✣ Nature: associations of the faithful are private (see canon 299 §2) or public (see canon 301 §3). They are distinguished from institutes of consecrated life and societies of apostolic life (see canon 298 §1) or, as a third order, they are under the direction of a religious institute (see canon 303).

✣ Purpose: the general purpose of associations is the perfection of charity (see canons 298 §1 and 303), by different means (see canons 298 §1, 301 §1, 303, 311, 327): promotion of public worship or Christian doctrine, activities of evangelization, works of piety or charity, animating the temporal order with a Christian spirit, and other spiritual ends.

✣ Members: associations can be composed (see canon 298 §1) of clerics (see canon 302) or laypeople (see canons 327–329). Being a mixed association, they can also group different believers in the same structure: clerics, laity, and religious (see canon 307 §3).

✣ Integration: the process of integration and dismissal must be carried out in accordance with the law and in accordance with the statutes of each association (see canons 307, 308, and 316). Validly admitted members enjoy the rights and privileges accorded to the association (see canon 306). The grounds for dismissal must be specified in the statutes, as well as the procedure and the competent body.[44]

✣ Government:[45] an association of the faithful is under the authority of a moderator (see canons 317, 321, and 324 §1), who directs it under regulated terms according to the

---

[44] See Lluís Martínez Sistach, *Las asociaciones de fieles* (Barcelona: Aranzadi, 1986), 105.

[45] Even if the General Decree *Associations of the Faithful* "disciplines the internal government of the international associations of the faithful, private and public, and of the other bodies with juridical personality subject to the direct supervision of the Dicastery for Laity, Family and Life" (*Explanatory Note*, no. 1), bishops can consider the opportunity to issue similar rules for associations in their respective areas of competence due to the reasonableness of the rules.

statutes[46] (see canon 304 §1), for the good of the members (see canon 329). Furthermore, rules must be established for the organization of assemblies, appointing directors, officers, ministers, or employees and administrators of property (see canons 309 and 319).

Belonging to an association with its pursuit of common goals can generate a sense of family and fraternity. In this context, the moderator's task is to build communion and the good of persons.

Finally, canon 304 §1 notes the seat of the association, which must be indicated in the statutes. It should not be understood as the canonical house of ordinary residence for its members. It is the legal seat which, in general, has the function of secretariat, archive, address for official correspondence and other letters, but also is a place that could serve for possible meetings.[47]

2. FRATERNAL LIFE BETWEEN DIFFERENT STATES OF LIFE[48]

New communities and *ecclesial movements* often have a mixed composition: laypeople—among whom some take the vows to observe the evangelical counsels privately—and clerics.[49] The members,

---

[46] It is necessary to regulate terms in the central governing body "in order to promote a healthy renewal and to prevent misappropriations that have indeed led to violations and abuses." Dicastery for Laity, Family, and Life, *Associations of the Faithful.* The *Explanatory Note,* no. 10, of this General Decree further asserts: "Experience has shown that a change in generations inside governing bodies through a rotation of responsibilities benefits the vitality of the association. It provides an opportunity for creative growth and stimulates investment in training. It reinvigorates faithfulness to the charism, breathes new life and efficacy to the interpretation of the signs of the times, and encourages new and updated paths of missionary action."

[47] See Martínez Sistach, *Las asociaciones de fieles,* 48.

[48] See *Iuvenescit Ecclesia,* in particular nos. 2 and 22.

[49] See Echeverría, "Los movimientos eclesiales," 578–580. See also Rose McDermott, "The Ninth Ordinary Session of the Synod of Bishops:

living an evangelical life, share the same charism and are at the service of a common ecclesial mission.[50] There is no doubt that this communion between laypeople and clerics can be a "helpful impulse to a renewed commitment by the Church in proclaiming and bearing witness to the Gospel of hope and charity in every corner of the world."[51]

It seems that "the discipline that canons 298–329 of the *Code of Canon Law* give to the associations of faithful is sufficiently flexible to permit the ecclesial movements [and new communities] to remain within this general category, but insufficient to regulate what is specific about them."[52] Indeed, some questions remain creating certain discomforts.

Four Moments and Six Canonical Issues," *Commentarium pro Religiosis et missionariis* 77 (1996): 279; Piero Coda, "The Ecclesial Movements, Gift of the Spirit: A Theological Reflection," in *Movements in the Church: Proceedings of the World Congress of the Ecclesial Movements, Rome, 27–29 May, 1998*, ed. Pontifical Council for the Laity (Vatican City: Pontificium Consilium pro Laicis, 1999), 93–95; "Dialogue with Joseph Card. Ratzinger," in *The Ecclesial Movements in the Pastoral Concern of the Bishops*, ed. Pontifical Council for the Laity (Vatican City: Pontificium Consilium pro Laicis, 2000), 229–230.

[50] See Miriam Kovač, "I consacrati e i movimenti ecclesiali," *Quaderni di diritto ecclesiale* 11 (1998): 86. Also: United States Conference of Catholic Bishops (USCCB), *Co-Workers in the Vineyard of the Lord: A Resource for Guiding the Development of Lay Ecclesial Ministry* (Washington, DC: USCCB Publishing, 2005), 19–20.

[51] Benedict XVI, Letter (June 16, 2009).

[52] Gianfranco Ghirlanda, "Charism and Juridical Status of the Ecclesial Movements," in *Movements in the Church: Proceedings of the World Congress of the Ecclesial Movements, Rome, 27–29 May, 1998*, ed. Pontifical Council for the Laity (Vatican City: Pontificium Consilium pro Laicis 1999), 131. See also Luís Navarro, "I nuovi movimenti ecclesiali nel magistero di Benedetto XVI," *Ius Ecclesiae* 21 (2009): 573. For some authors the current codification is not adapted: Dortel-Claudot, "Les communautés nouvelles," 6; Silvia Recchi, "I movimenti ecclesiali e l'incardinazione dei sacerdoti membri," *Quaderni di diritto ecclesiale* 15 (2002): 175. See also Hegge, "I movimenti ecclesiali," 515–517.

For example, who will be responsible for the formation of future clerics[53] and what level of authority do they have over those incardinated in a diocese or in another particular church?[54] Insofar as the associations do not require total dedication to their works, a double belonging could be compatible: the spirituality and fraternity of the association are a support for priestly spirituality and communion in the presbytery.

However, it seems less obvious to find adjustments between belonging to a particular church and at the same time being committed to associations that demand a more complete dedication from their members. Incardination creates a canonical bond between the ordained minister and the diocese. This issue can be resolved through agreements between the diocesan bishop and the association's moderator. It is hoped, however, that the Ordinary and his successors would be generous in allowing the incardinated cleric to serve the needs of his association.

Another question arises when it comes to enrolling members of institutes of consecrated life or societies of apostolic life in this type of association. These already have an identity formed by their particular heritage: each institute of consecrated life and society of apostolic life has its own requirements. It seems,

---

[53] The "Norms for Priestly Formation" established by the competent ecclesiastical authority must be followed (see canon 242). Normally, this formation takes place in the major seminary (see canon 235 §1), but "the diocesan bishop is to entrust those who legitimately reside outside a seminary to a devout and suitable priest who is to be watchful that they are carefully formed in the spiritual life and in discipline" (canon 235 §2). For religious, "universal law and the program of studies proper to the institute govern the formation of members who are preparing to receive holy orders" (canon 659 §3).

[54] It is important to recall, in fact, that "every cleric must be incardinated either in a particular church or personal prelature, or in an institute of consecrated life or society endowed with this faculty, in such a way that unattached or transient clerics are not allowed at all" (canon 265).

therefore, a challenge to reconcile them with new rules of fraternal communion. For solitary forms of consecrated life—as in the case of the order of virgins—the difficulties are analogous to those evoked for clerics. On the other hand, one can ask what formation is proposed or what disciplinary framework is offered to members who privately adopt the evangelical counsels.

Furthermore, there is the issue of governing authority.[55] In a mixed association, composed of laypeople and clergy, the statutes may allow the supreme moderator to be chosen from either vocation. When a priest is under the authority of a layperson, the question arises as to what authority a lay moderator can have over a priest and his ministry. Especially when associative commitments demand total availability, it is difficult to dissociate the observance of these commitments from the demands of the ordained ministry itself.

In order for priests to be under the responsibility of an ordained minister, some associations provide for a priest general councilor together with the moderator. His function is to manage the selection and training of candidates along with guiding the practice of ordained ministry. But such a disposition is not without tension, especially in conflict situations: the tendency is not to turn to the lay moderator, but frequently resort to the bishop of incardination, whose neutrality of interest is not always assured.

---

[55] For a deeper analysis of this problem, see Luigi Sabbarese, "L'autorità nelle nuove comunità," in *Nuove forme di vita consacrata*, ed. R. Fusco and G. Rocca, 91–112 (Rome: Urbaniana University Press, 2010).

CHAPTER IV

STATES OF LIFE

THE SPECIFIC VOCATION OF THE LAITY

1. PEOPLE OF GOD: EQUAL DIGNITY IN DIVERSITY

THE CONCILIAR MAGISTERIUM GAVE precedence to the People of God as a whole. The Council recognized believers or Christians (*christi-fideles*) as the subject of the mission by highlighting their fundamental and common character: configuration to Christ by Baptism. Thus, all of Jesus' disciples have equal dignity. The Council also preserved the traditional tripartite classification of clerics—consecrated—lay-people, which had already entered into the 1917 *Code*.[56] It is a practical synthesis for understanding the vocation proper to particular groups or orders of people who, in the communion of the Church, constitute the People of God.[57] Let us recall some specific aspects.

---

[56] Clerics are bishops, priests, and deacons. Laypeople: married and celibate. Consecrated: religious, members of secular institutes, hermits, consecrated virgins, consecrated widows, members of new forms of consecrated life.

[57] It is a practical synthesis: on the one hand, *clerics* and *laity* (these are all those who have not received Holy Orders, whether a mother of a family or a Carmelite); on the other hand, *consecrated* and *non-consecrated* (these are those who do not profess the evangelical counsels in a form of consecrated life, such as *secular clergy* and *laity* in general; *consecrated*

What characterizes an ordained minister? By virtue of his sacred ordination, the baptized person receives a *new sacramental consecration that ontologically configures him to the Christ-Head.* Through the ministerial priesthood "it is Christ himself who is present to his Church as Head of his Body, Shepherd of his flock, high priest of the redemptive sacrifice, Teacher of Truth.... The priest, by virtue of the sacrament of Holy Orders, acts *in persona Christi Capitis*—in the person of Christ the Head."[58]

This consecration is not an honor that is received for a particular merit: "It depends entirely on Christ and on his unique priesthood; it has been instituted for the good of men and the communion of the Church [and] ... must therefore be measured against the model of Christ, who by love made himself the least and the servant of all."[59] Indeed,

> This presence of Christ in the minister is not to be understood as if the latter were preserved from all human weaknesses, the spirit of domination, error, even sin. The power of the Holy Spirit does not guarantee all acts of ministers in the same way. While this guarantee extends to the sacraments, so that even the minister's sin cannot impede the fruit of grace, in many other acts the minister leaves human traces that are not always signs of fidelity to the Gospel and consequently can harm the apostolic fruitfulness of the Church.[60]

We can ask ourselves what, in turn, characterizes the consecrated life? This is "the state of life which is constituted by the profession

---

persons are those who live in a form of consecrated life, and may be clergy or laity in the sense of non-clergy).

[58] *CCC*, no. 1548.

[59] Ibid., no. 1551.

[60] Ibid., no. 1550.

of the evangelical counsels."[61] The baptized person does not enter the consecrated life through a new sacramental consecration: "In the consecrated life, Christ's faithful, moved by the Holy Spirit, propose to follow Christ more nearly, to give themselves to God who is loved above all and, pursuing the perfection of charity in the service of the Kingdom, to signify and proclaim in the Church the glory of the world to come."[62]

In the consecrated life, one seeks to live in baptismal grace and dedicates oneself totally to God. Since all the faithful are called to holiness, that is, to the perfection of charity, the consecrated person does so in a specific way: through the profession of the evangelical counsels in a stable state of life recognized by the Church.[63] Thus, "the perfection of charity, to which all the faithful are called, entails for those who freely follow the call to consecrated life the obligation of practicing chastity in celibacy for the sake of the Kingdom, poverty and obedience."[64]

Coming to the definition of layperson, the *Catechism of the Catholic Church*, no. 897 states:

> The term "laity" is here understood to mean all the faithful except those in Holy Orders and those who belong to a religious state approved by the Church. That is, the faithful, who by Baptism are incorporated into Christ and integrated into the People of God, are made sharers in their particular way in the priestly, prophetic, and kingly office of Christ, and have their

---

[61] Ibid., no. 914.

[62] Ibid., no. 916.

[63] These stable forms are: the hermit's life, the order of consecrated virgins, consecrated widowhood, religious institutes, secular institutes, the new forms of consecrated life according to canon 605 and, in a certain way, the Societies of Apostolic Life.

[64] *CCC*, no. 915.

own part to play in the mission of the whole Christian people in the Church and in the World.

Finally, the definition of the laity—of its deep being—coincides with the general description of the baptized and, negatively, as non-ordained and non-consecrated. Laypeople have neither received the ordained ministry nor professed the evangelical counsels in a form of consecrated life recognized by the Church. Unlike the call to the priesthood or to the consecrated life, which are marked, one by a sacrament of the Church, the other by the rite of profession, the *laity* does not involve a call from God to become lay.

The constitution *Lumen gentium*, no. 31, which the *Catechism* mentions, states that "what specifically characterizes the laity is their secular nature." What does this mean? What is the relevance of secularity for those who are linked, for example, to a new community and who are particularly involved in its own works? Does the charism of a new association help laypeople to be "more secular"?

2. The Secularity of the Laity and the New Associations[65]

2.1 *The Second Vatican Council*

Who is the layperson? What is his specificity? What does he do in a new community?

Thanks to the development of the lay apostolate in the first half of the twentieth century, the Magisterium's interventions prepared, in a way, theological reflection on the laity.[66] Then comes

---

[65] See CNBB, *Mission and Ministries of Lay Christians* (Itaici: Editora Paulinas, 1999), particularly nos. 99–110. Also *Co-Workers in the Vineyard of the Lord*, 8–9.

[66] The first major intervention of the Magisterium was made by Leo XIII. See also Pius XI, Encyclical Letter *Ubi arcano Dei consilio* on the Peace

the question of the *proprium*-characteristic of the laity in the Church. This is an ecclesiological question: What is the theological value of the notion of the laity?

We have seen that the Second Vatican Council highlights the notion of *christifideles* (*Christian faithful*). Some awkwardness exists in giving a definition of a layperson. In fact, in conciliar works, the notion of the layperson is sometimes simply identified with the notion of the faithful. In fact, it was even proposed to suppress it.[67] Finally, although present in *Lumen gentium*, no. 31 and proposed in the decrees *Apostolicam actuositatem*, *Gaudium et spes*, and *Ad gentes*, this notion expresses not a dogmatic and theological definition of the layperson, but a typological and sociological description.[68]

Indeed, "the main concern of the Council ... was of an apostolic nature; it did not want to answer the question who is the laity, but what kind of presence and activity laypeople can have in the mission of the Church."[69] More than a notion, the Council

of Christ in the Kingdom of Christ (December 23, 1922); Pius XII: *Potenza e influsso della Chiesa* (February 20, 1946); Apostolic Constitution *Provida Mater Ecclesia* concerning Secular Institutes (February 2, 1947); Motu Proprio *Primo feliciter* (March 12, 1948); Apostolic Constitution *Bis saeculari die* on Marian Congregations (September 27, 1948). One may refer to *Actes du premier congrès mondial pour l'Apostolat des Laïcs en 1951* and *Documents du deuxième congrès mondial pour l'Apostolat des Laïcs en 1957*.

[67] See Adolfo Longhitano, "Laico, persona, fedele cristiano. Quale categoria giuridica fondamentale per i battezzati?," in *Il fedele cristiano. La condizione giuridica dei battezzati*, ed. A. Longhitano (Bologna: EDB, 1989), 17–23. See also Second Vatican Council, *Acta Synodalia Sacrosancti Concilii Oecumenici Vaticani II* Periodus prima, pars IV. Typis Polyglottis Vaticanus, 1971: 155.

[68] It is in these terms that the *Relatio* is expressed in no. 31: see Second Vatican Council, *Acta Synodalia* III/1: 282. See also Edward Schillebeeckx, "Definizione del laico cristiano," in *La Chiesa del Vaticano II*, ed. G. Baraúna, (Florence: Vallecchi, 1965).

[69] Eugenio Zanetti, "I laici," in *Fedeli, Associazioni, Movimenti*, ed. Gruppo Italiano Docenti di Diritto Canonico (Milan: Edizioni glossa,

developed an aspect of the layperson's mission. Furthermore, in treating the issue of advancement of temporal realities as something specific to laypeople, the Council recognizes the secular dimension as representing the whole Church.

The Council explicitly stated that the secular dimension is not reserved for the laity[70] and the *proprium* of the laity is never exclusively attributed to them.[71] In fact, by establishing a parallel with other vocations, the Council recognizes that the apostolate of the laity is more linked to temporal affairs because normally laypeople find themselves *more than others* in relation to different conditions of family and social life (see *Lumen gentium*, no. 31). Thus, secularity is not a theological criterion to exclusively characterize a category of the baptized, the laity.

2.2 THE CODE OF CANON LAW

Reflection on the notion of the layperson in legislative texts benefited from post-conciliar reflection. The group in charge of drafting a definition of the laypeople soon abandoned the project in favor of the centrality of the notion of the *Christian faithful* (*christifideles*).

2002), 41 (my translation).

[70] One can read: "Secular duties and activities belong properly although not exclusively to laymen." Second Vatican Council, Pastoral Constitution *Gaudium et spes* on the Church in the Modern World (December 7, 1965), no. 43. In fact, "it is evident that every member of God's people has, like the Church itself, a secular character." Armando Oberti, "Les Instituts séculiers dans le nouveau code de droit canonique," *Vies consacrée* 55 (1983) : 211.

[71] This is the case of *Lumen gentium*, no. 31. Even if the secular dimension is indicated as *propria et peculiaris*, the text immediately adds: "It is true that those in Holy Orders can at times be engaged in secular activities, and even have a secular profession. But they are by reason of their particular vocation especially and professedly ordained to the sacred ministry." It is also the thought of *Christifideles laici*, no. 15.

The first formulations of the term *laity* make reference to Baptism, Confirmation, and participation in the Church's mission. All these elements are constitutive of the notion of *christifideles*. Considering the difficulty of defining the layperson autonomously from the notion of the faithful, the legislator refrained from giving a specific definition of the layperson—defining only the notion of the faithful in canon 204 §1—without even proposing the conciliar typological description. [72] The layperson is presented simply as a non-cleric: "By divine institution, there are among the Christian faithful in the Church sacred ministers who in law are also called clerics; the other members of the Christian faithful are called lay persons" (canon 207 §1).

If the drafters of the *Code* were "obliged" to write their own canons for laypeople, they did so for essentially psychological reasons. [73] In fact, they said: "It is difficult to make a special section for the laity other than the *christifideles*. In fact, all the rights and duties of the faithful are also those of lay people, since the majority

[72] The canon says: "The Christian faithful are those who, inasmuch as they have been incorporated in Christ through baptism, have been constituted as the people of God. For this reason, made sharers in their own way in Christ's priestly, prophetic, and royal function, they are called to exercise the mission which God has entrusted to the Church to fulfill in the world, in accord with the condition proper to each."

[73] Seven canons list the rights and duties of laypeople: canons 225–231. However, at least six can be attributed to all the faithful (laity, clerics, consecrated persons): canons 225 §1 (first part); 229 §§1–3; 231 §§1–2. Six other canons can also be attributed to the lay faithful, whether they live in the world or are members of institutes of consecrated life or societies of apostolic life: canons 225 §1 (second part); 228 §§1–2; 230 §§1–3. The three rights and duties assigned to married laypeople in canon 226 also apply to married clerics (permanent deacons). If we consider the secular character as proper to the laity, there are two specific rights and duties: the duty to imbue the temporal order with the spirit of the Gospel (canon 225 §2) and the right to exercise this mission freely (canon 227).

of the faithful are lay people. However, it seems opportune, even on the psychological level, to have particular canons on lay people."[74] Hence, there is no fundamental difference between the layperson and the faithful: laypersons are *christifideles* who, in very different situations, live in the Church and in the world.

2.3 OPEN HORIZON

Seeking an element proper to the layperson, the Council indicated secularity as specific to its apostolate. With similar terms, the *Code* proposes this idea in canon 225 §2.[75] The pontifical Magisterium took up the concept.[76] But a definition of layperson whose content was of a theological nature was not given.[77]

In fact, *secularity* is not an ontological element that contributes to the theological definition of the layperson. If so, its origin remains to be proved. If secularity were to derive from Baptism, then all the baptized — clerics and consecrated persons included — would have it as their own element. If it came from a charism, what is its nature?[78] When do you receive it? Who discerns it and how? It seems, therefore, that the notion of secularity is a simple sociological and typological, if not pastoral element, since laypeople often lead ordinary lives in

---

[74] *Communicationes*, 13 (1981), 314 (my translation).

[75] Laypeople "are also bound by a particular duty to imbue and perfect the order of temporal affairs with the spirit of the gospel and thus to give witness to Christ, especially in carrying out these same affairs and in exercising secular functions."

[76] See, for example, *Christifideles laici*, no. 15.

[77] *Christifideles laici* contains a paragraph entitled "Who are the Lay Faithful" (no. 9). However, instead of offering a definition of a layperson or talking about his identity, the text will only give a description of what characterizes him in general. See also no. 15 of this document.

[78] See José Luis Illanes, "La discusión teológica sobre la noción de laico," *Scripta theologica* 22 (1990): 771–789.

the world.[79] The *saeculum*, that is, the *world*, is not the domain of exclusive competence of laypeople. But "the relationship with the world ... characterizes all the baptized.... The entire community of believers is challenged by the *saeculum*, even if some have a particular relationship with it.... Each one is called to have a relationship with the realities of the world, in accordance with the charismatic and ministerial *proprium* that characterizes him."[80] There is only one apostolate, one mission of the Church in the world. The National Conference of Bishops of Brazil document *Lay Christians in Church and Society*, no. 4 says it succinctly:

> The Church-world dichotomy persists, many times, as a position both for those who dispense with the Church at the time of living as a social and political subject, and for those who dispense with the world in their experiences and actions within the Church.[81]

The *secular* is, therefore, an instance internal to the Christian novelty and not a temporal or historical condition outside the Church.[82]

---

[79] See Longhitano, "Laico, persona, fedele cristiano," 27–28. See also Luís Navarro, "Lo statuto giuridico del laico: Sacerdozio comune e secolarità," *Fidelium iura* 7 (1997) : 88–94, and Marc Ouellet, *L'apport des mouvements ecclésiaux: Unité et diversité dans l'Esprit* (Bruyères-le-Châtel: Nouvelle Cité, 2011), 77–89.

[80] Bruno Forte, *Laicato e laicità: Saggi ecclesiologici* (Casale Monferrato: Marietti, 1986), 46 (my translation). See also Gianfranco Ghirlanda, "Consilia evangelica in vita laicali," *Periodica* 87 (1998): 569.

[81] The National Conference of Bishops of Brazil, *Lay Christians in Church and Society*, (São Paulo: Editora Paulinas: 2016), no. 4.

[82] See Ghirlanda, "Consilia evangelica in vita laicali," 570. We can read in *Consecration and Secularity*: "In life, however, there is no such thing as a space for the sacred and another for the profane; a time for God and a time for the small or big events of history." Congregation for Institutes of Consecrated Life and Societies of Apostolic Life, Letter

The notion of the layperson would be compromised if Baptism were not the primordial reference, which ontologically configures him to Christ, priest, prophet, and king. The central place of Baptism and the category of *christifideles* are the fundamental theological elements to be considered, as they define the entire People of God. [83] In this way one can better understand all the successive diversifications (*christifideles*-laity, *christifideles*-clergy, *christifideles*-consecrated), which manifest the action of the Church's unique mission. [84] In this context, the specificity of laypeople is not limited to secularity: their mission is carried out in the Church and in the world, through different actions and ministries that are not ordained, alone or associated. Even if, as Pope Francis says:

> A clear awareness of this responsibility of the laity, grounded in their baptism and confirmation, does not appear in the same way in all places. In some cases, it is because lay persons have not been given the formation needed to take on important responsibilities. In others, it is because in their particular Churches room

---

Consecration and Secularity to the Bishops of the Catholic Church Regarding the Secular Institutes (June 4, 2017), no. 3.

[83] "Who is a layperson? As a first answer, one might be tempted to say: every baptized person, who from his profane state was called by Christ in his holy Church, who in the sacrament of Baptism was buried with him (Rom. 6:4), who with him rose to a new divine life (Eph. 2:6). All Christians, who belong to the holy people (*laos*), would have the right to be honored with the title of *layperson*: the pope, bishops, priests, just as the Christian who lives in the married state and exercises a profane profession. However, a long tradition does not allow us to use the word *layperson* in this way: all those who belong to the holy people are designated by the name of the *faithful*." Hans Urs von Balthasar, "Chi è un laico?," *Communio* 83/84 (1985): 4.

[84] "Laity, as well as sacred ministers ..., are above all *christifideles* and participate in the common condition of all the members of the people of God." *Communicationes* 2 (1979): 89.

has not been made for them to speak and to act, due to an excessive clericalism which keeps them away from decision-making.[85]

This notion of laity raises another question: What is the specificity of lay members involved in a movement or new community? And could this way of life be distinguished by a deeper secularity? I don't think so. In fact, laypeople who belong to a new association are called to live their baptismal consecration according to the charism they freely adhere to as a concrete means of responding to the universal call to holiness. This vocation is lived in an association of the faithful that tends "to foster a more perfect life, to promote public worship or Christian doctrine, or to exercise other works of the apostolate such as initiatives of evangelization, works of piety or charity, and those which animate the temporal order with a Christian spirit" (canon 298 §1).

[85] *Evangelii gaudium*, no. 102.

CHAPTER V

CONSECRATION

EVANGELICAL COUNSELS AND VOWS[86]

1. THE TERM CONSECRATION

THE WORD "CONSECRATION" is often used loosely. For example: "I am consecrated to such a movement or community." Every Christian is consecrated thanks to the gift of the sacrament of Baptism.[87] In fact, it can be said that every human being is *religious* because he seeks — in different ways — to *reconnect* with the divine.

Monsignor Miguel Delgado Galindo, under-secretary of the former Pontifical Council for the Laity, warns however:

> The broad meaning [of the word *consecration*] has meant that it is used in different ways and sometimes inappropriately, often causing confusion. Regularly the members of ecclesial movements ... that adopt the evangelical counsels are called "consecrated" or

---

[86] See the articles Recchi, "Per una configurazione canonica dei movimenti ecclesiali"; Barbara Zadra, "L'assunzione dei consigli evangelici negli statuti delle associazioni che prevedono la consacrazione di vita," *Quaderni di diritto ecclesiale* 12 (1999): 353–362; Echeverría, "Los movimientos eclesiales."

[87] See *Compendium of the Catechism of the Catholic Church*, no. 589.

"consecrated lay."... The fact [that lay people] adopt the evangelical counsels has convinced several authors ... to consider them as consecrated, giving rise to numerous misunderstandings that we see daily. For lay people who adopt the evangelical counsels in ecclesial movements there is no new consecration.... Consequently, these lay people are not "consecrated" faithful, since what characterizes consecrated life is the profession of the evangelical counsels ... in an institute of consecrated life recognized as such by the competent authority of the Church.[88]

The author's position, which, moreover, has particular relevance given the fact that he was under-secretary of the former Pontifical Council for the Laity, seems evident regarding the misuse of the word *consecrated*. Terminological clarity is a service that is available to everyone: "A uniform terminology and a lack of adequate information can mislead people who take up the evangelical counsels, in associations or movements, and who live in a true and proper form of recognized consecrated life recognized by the Church, without actually assuming the consequences that this entails and without having the protection that the Church offers to the state of consecrated life."[89]

Furthermore, the indistinct use of words in certain contexts, including ecclesial ones, can make them lose their original meaning: from the Council, through the *Code of Canon Law* and the pontifical Magisterium, *consecrated* is the one who integrated the canonical state of consecrated life in one of the approved forms

[88] Miguel Delgado Galindo, "Le don de soi dans les mouvements ecclésiaux" (lecture at the Study Day on "Consecration in Ecclesial Movements and in New Communities—Theological and Juridical Aspects," Budapest, April 25, 2009).

[89] Ghirlanda, "Consilia evangelica in vita laicali," 585 (my translation).

(see the schema below). *Religious*, in the ecclesial sphere, is the consecrated member of a religious institute. In summary:

Consecrated life distinguished in:

Collective forms: — Religious — Secular Institutes — Ecclesial Families

Individual forms: — Hermits — Virgins — Widows

All of these collective and individual forms are canonically consecrated because they profess — by vows or other sacred bonds — the evangelical counsels of chastity, poverty, and obedience, in a state of canonically consecrated life erected by the competent authority of the Church (see canon 573 §2).

Of course, these evangelical counsels can be lived outside the consecrated life. However, by decision of the Church, their experience does not confer a particular ecclesial status. In fact, the will of ecclesiastical authority is constitutive of the reality we call "consecrated life." Its action, juridical or liturgical, declares it authentic, publicly recognizes it, and gives it canonical existence as a state of life.

2. CHASTITY, POVERTY, AND OBEDIENCE

Pope John Paul II, in his apostolic exhortation *Vita consecrata*, made us understand that the so-called "evangelical counsels" are attitudes proper to Christ, or rather, they constitute His profound being as Son of the Father. Nailed to the Cross, "his virginal love for the Father and for all mankind will attain its highest expression. His poverty will reach complete self-emptying, his obedience the giving of his life."[90] Jesus loves uniquely. He depends entirely on His Father

---

[90] John Paul II, Apostolic Exhortation *Vita consecrata* on the Consecrated Life and Its Mission in the Church and in the World (March 25, 1996), no. 23.

in Heaven, and His freedom is in deep communion with the One who sent Him.

John Paul II goes even further when he affirms that the evangelical counsels of chastity, poverty, and obedience are lived in the very heart of the Holy Trinity:

> The *chastity* of celibates and virgins, ... is a reflection of the *infinite love* which links the three Divine Persons in the mysterious depths of the life of the Trinity.... *Poverty* proclaims that God is man's only real treasure ..., an expression of that *total gift of self* which the three Divine Persons make to one another.... *Obedience*, ... shows the liberating beauty of a *dependence which is not servile but filial*, marked by a deep sense of responsibility and animated by mutual trust, which is a reflection in history of the loving *harmony* between the three Divine Persons. The consecrated life is thus called constantly to deepen the gift of the evangelical counsels with a love which grows ever more genuine and strong in the *Trinitarian* dimension.... The consecrated life thus becomes a confession and a sign of the Trinity. [91]

Within the Church, some people follow Christ more radically by living like He did on earth. They do this through the profession of the evangelical counsels "by which the faithful, following Christ more closely under the action of the Holy Spirit, are totally dedicated to God who is loved most of all, so that, having been dedicated by a new and special title to His honor, to the building up of the Church, and to the salvation of the world, they strive for the perfection of charity in the service of the kingdom of God and, having been made an outstanding sign in the Church, foretell the heavenly glory. [They] freely assume this form of living in

[91] *Vita consecrata*, no. 21.

institutes of consecrated life canonically erected by competent authority of the Church" (canon 573).

And yet, the spirit of the evangelical counsels applies to all Christians. In fact, all are called by Christ to chastity, which finds in God the fullness of love; to poverty, which reminds us that our treasure must be in Heaven; to obedience, which invites us to listen to His words and put them into practice. Since these counsels are lived in Trinitarian communion as Pope John Paul II reminded us, each citizen of Heaven lives them out fully because God is all in all.

On earth, some embrace the practice of the evangelical counsels while others must live their spirit. Everyone hopes to live them to the full at the end of time. This justifies the use of chastity, poverty, and obedience in many associations when describing the commitments of their members.

In movements and new communities, as far as chastity is concerned, it is obvious what chastity in Catholic marriage entails. Sometimes couples "confirm by means of a vow the obligation of chastity proper to the married state."[92] It is also evident what chastity is for celibates, lived in continence as a natural virtue. Some of them assume it perpetually. Experience shows us that the lay faithful can assume in ecclesial movements (as well as outside associative realities) the commitment to live apostolic celibacy. John Paul II writes that within the lay state of life there is room for various vocations, that is, different spiritual and apostolic paths.[93]

As for poverty, it should be said that couples, even assuming the "spirit of poverty," must not neglect "their duties towards their children."[94] This implies not only ensuring an education imbued

---

[92] *Vita consecrata*, no. 62.
[93] See *Christifideles laici*, no. 56.
[94] *Vita consecrata*, no. 62.

with the Catholic Faith, but also—depending on the social context in which they live—a certain quality of life and the means to forge a perspective of the future (education, professionalization, opening to the world of work, etc.). As for celibates who intend to persevere in this way, "prudence demands that the norms that govern every renunciation should not be stricter than those that apply to perpetually professed members of religious institutes."[95]

In the experience of obedience, lay associations ask their members for the necessary availability to exercise the apostolate common to all. Participation varies according to the degree of belonging and commitment. As stated in the aforementioned document by the *Conseil Permanent de l'Épiscopat Français* on the drafting of the statutes of the new communities, it is worth remembering the need to preserve the indispensable autonomy of families, so that parents exercise the inalienable responsibility in the education of their children.

3. Meaning of Vows

A vow is the deliberate and free promise made to God of a possible and better good, which must be fulfilled by reason of the virtue of religion (see canon 1191 §1). In the vow, the promise is made to God; it is an act of *latria*—supreme homage—and therefore it has its source in the virtue of religion, and in the love that one has for God. Through the vow, the person responds to a divine vocation: the recipient of the vow is God. The obligation to fulfill the vow fully and faithfully springs from charity and the response to the divine vocation is carried out in love.

In consecrated life vows are public, as "a legitimate superior accepts it in the name of the Church" (canon 1192 §1). As a general

---

[95] Conseil Permanent de l'Épiscopat Français, *Points de repère proposés aux évêques de France pour accompagner une communauté nouvelle. Notamment lors de l'élaboration de ses statuts* (June 17, 1987) (my translation).

rule, vows are taken during a liturgical celebration, in which the Church mediates through the presence of the legitimate superior who dialogues with the candidate and accepts his firm resolution. Likewise, in order to obtain a dispensation from vows, the Church's mediation is necessary, proceeding in accordance with the norms of canon law (see canons 686–704; 726–730; 742–746).

Any vows made in the new associations are considered private, in accordance with canon 1192 §1, even if they were taken in front of a group of people or an assembly. Commitments made by members are not received by the moderator on the Church's behalf. It would, therefore, be opportune for the assumption of evangelical counsels in movements and new communities not to be accepted by the moderator, in order to avoid interpreting it as a public profession of the evangelical counsels (see canon 1192 §1).

Whatever it is, making a vow, even private, has an undeniable legal value. The person bound by the vow cannot invoke the Name of God in vain in such a serious circumstance in terms of the commitment that is assumed and must faithfully fulfill the promise made. This juridical act is so important and serious that the dispensation from the vow is regulated by canon 1196, in which the necessary intervention of the Church's mediation is affirmed: "In addition to the Roman Pontiff, the following can dispense from private vows for a just cause ...: the local ordinary and the pastor with regard to all their subjects and even travelers," that is, to those who are just passing through the territory. Of course, if the dispensation of the vows meant separation from the association, the statutes could specify that such dispensation would be worthless without the agreement of the moderator general.[96]

---

[96] See Jean Beyer, "Vita associativa e corresponsabilità ecclesiale," *Vita consacrata* 26 (1990): 935.

As alluded to earlier, people who adopt the evangelical counsels by vows or other promises in ecclesial movements and new communities do not change their state of life. Therefore, from the canonical perspective, they are not "consecrated." In fact, "the only consecration they received was the one common to all Christians, which is conferred on them by the sacraments of Baptism, Confirmation and, in the case of clerics, by Holy Orders. It must be stated clearly that consecrated life is that of a state that one lives in an institute canonically erected by the competent authority of the Church."[97]

<hr/>

[97] Delgado Galindo, *Le don de soi*.

CHAPTER VI

COMMUNITY LIFE

Family Spirit[98]

---

1. Communion in Diversity

The notion of *communion*[99] applied to the Church evokes the personal union of the baptized with the Holy Trinity and with their brothers and sisters in the Faith. This communion exists already on earth and guides the Church towards eschatological fullness. Different ecclesial institutions and associations share this grace of communion, making it present and operative: the diocese, parish communities, institutes of consecrated life, and associations. In this way "one heart and mind" are built (Acts 4:32) and one is at the service of communion, announcing and witnessing to the mystery that constitutes the Church.

In many communities a family spirit reigns, where relationships are warm and simple. However, one should not confuse a

---

[98] This chapter is essentially inspired by Tony Anatrella's book: *Développer la vie communautaire dans l'Église*, especially from pages 107–251.

[99] See *Lumen gentium*, nos. 4, 8, 13–15, 18, 21, 24–25; Second Vatican Council, Dogmatic Constitution *Dei Verbum* on Divine Revelation (November 18, 1965), no. 10; *Gaudium et spes*, no. 32; Second Vatican Council, Decree *Unitatis redintegratio* on Ecumenism (November 21, 1964), nos. 2–4, 14–15, 17–19, 22.

community that has its own synergy with a family that, in itself, has characteristics that are unique and that are not comparable. The family is founded on the choice of a man and a woman and their procreation, which together constitute the familial bond, while the group is constituted from a charism, which gathers and guides its reason for being and its historical development.

In a Catholic association, the lifestyle depends on its spiritual purpose. The personal affective life must be inscribed in this context, balanced by the virtue of chastity, and submitted to the evangelical life. Even if a group has a family style of life lived out in a simple fraternal way, life in this group has nothing to do with conjugal life. In a community this type of relationship alters its nature and destroys its identity, for the sexual expression is reserved to husband and wife, to reinforce their union as a married couple.

Thus, when an association brings together clergy and laity, married or single men and women, it is important to emphasize balanced and healthy relationships. In fact, the enthusiasm to live the gospel together must account for the sociological laws inherent in every human reality so that the ideal of community can be realized. It is not enough to simply say that a group lives a fraternal relationship in order to neutralize the attractiveness that normally exists between men and women.

2. Pitfalls to Be Avoided

Some "diseases" can always ruin an initially healthy charism. Pope Francis affirms that "all ecclesial realities are called to conversion,"[100] for these diseases can affect them all with greater or lesser intensity.

---

[100] Francis, Address (September 16, 2021), no. 5.

Lust for Power

"The ... lust for power makes [one] change the nature of service in governance.... Our desire for power is expressed in many ways in the life of the Church; for example, when we believe, by virtue of the role we have, that we have to take decisions on all aspects of the life of our association.... We delegate tasks and responsibilities for certain areas to others, but only in theory! In practice, however, delegation to others is emptied by the eagerness to be everywhere. And this desire for power nullifies all forms of subsidiarity."[101]

Disloyalty

"We encounter [disloyalty] when someone wants to serve the Lord but also serves other things that are not the Lord.... We say in words that we want to serve God and others, but in fact we serve our ego, and we bend to our desire to appear, to obtain recognition, appreciation.... Let us not forget that true service is gratuitous and unconditional, it knows no calculations or demands.... We fall into the trap of disloyalty when we present ourselves to others as the sole interpreters of the charism, the sole heirs of our association or movement ... or when, believing ourselves to be indispensable, we do all we can to hold posts for life; or again when we claim to decide *a priori* who our successor should be."[102]

Self-referentiality

"Not infrequently, for those called to govern, the absence of limits in terms of office favors forms of appropriation of the charism, personalization, centralization and expressions of self-referentiality which can easily cause serious violations of personal dignity and freedom, and even real abuses. Furthermore, bad government

[101] Ibid.
[102] Ibid., no. 6.

inevitably creates conflicts and tensions which injure communion and weaken missionary dynamism."[103]

Clericalism

"Spiritual or conscience abuse is spiritual harassment, manipulation of consciences, brainwashing. This type of abuse usually occurs in areas of spiritual direction or within a community, especially when the internal forum is not distinguished from the external one. In general terms, we can say that it is the abuse of 'clericalism,' knowing that said abuse is not only typical of clerics, but also of other people with authority, be they men or women."[104]

Sectarianism

"Sectarianism usually manifests itself in the fundamentalist and ideological defense of the charism to preserve it from possible contamination that may come from outside. In groups in which a 'sectarian drift' can be observed, the mentality that 'we are the best,' that we are the only faithful ones is favored. This leads to the group becoming closed and setting up barriers of all kinds against possible harmful influences. In groups like this, it is also thought that the charism belongs to the founders and not to the Church, the only one to which its recognition and accompaniment really belong."[105]

---

[103] General Decree *Associations of the Faithful, Explanatory Note*, no. 9.

[104] This text is my translation of José Rodríguez Carballo, "El Vaticano está investigando a una decena de fundadores por abusos o gestión económica," interview by Darío Menor, *Vida Nueva*, July 30, 2021, https://www.vidanuevadigital.com/2021/07/30/jose-rodriguez-carballo-el-vaticano -esta-investigando-a-una-decena-de-fundadores-por-abusos-o-gestion-economica/

[105] Ibid.

Transparency

Transparency, which consists in expressing one's expectations to another, is not a recommended attitude. The spontaneous expression of something that is perceived is not in itself a value in community and social life. It is necessary to analyze the situation, without attributing any intuition or simple self-suggestions as promptings of the Holy Spirit.

Neediness

Neediness is another attitude that manifests itself in relationships. It is a way of pleasing the other to retain you. Thus, immature personalities will tend to seek recognition and appreciation from a person, for example, who has authority. This kind of affective gratification, very childish and adolescent, is sought after. In a community you cannot have such expectations.

Fusional Relationship

A fusional relationship is a possible feature of community functioning. The need to commit to a common project can be confused with the desire to simply be together, similar to teenagers hanging out. "Charism" and "good feelings" are confused, purely from the affective and emotional aspect. In a community, the communion that takes place through the mediation of Christ must be promoted. The role of authority is fundamental, to make the group evolve from a fusional relationship to a relationship of otherness.

Inbred Relationship

Inbreeding, in this context, is to entertain affective and sentimental relationships, even a certain sex trade, with people belonging to the religious group, when the latter has no such purpose. In such a relationship, sentimental effusions and undue attractions are manifested. Thus, the community's deviation of meaning is particularly serious.

Eroticization of Relationships

Two excesses in the new associations should be avoided: on the one hand, fear of the other sex, and on the other, relational naïveté, imprudence, and trivialization of gestures. It is not because you have a spiritual life that you can allow all sensible expressions, even disinterested ones. The fact of spiritualizing certain gestures and affective demonstrations does not integrate the reality of sexual impulses, running the risk of turning against people and creating a harmful climate in the community.

3. COMMUNITY MATURITY CRITERIA[106]

Sometimes certain confusions in the community can arise. A community is built around an evangelical project of holiness, including a social commitment to works of charity and mercy, not as a result of affective expectations.[107]

A community that is built on affective expectations, if it does not evolve, will weaken over time. Relational proximity and affective immaturity predominate, without being based on objective criteria for evaluating community life. It is not because one lives in community and in the name of a shared "fraternity" that feelings and emotions should be shared. Relationships become particularly complicated when they are predominantly founded on affective interests.

A community whose solid foundation is an evangelical project of holiness will have other requirements as a rule, without

---

[106] See the important "Criteria for Discerning the Charismatic Gifts" in *Iuvenescit Ecclesia*, no. 18, for example: communion with the Church, the presence of spiritual fruits, the social dimension of evangelization, esteem for other charisms, and the confession of the Catholic Faith. The Canadian Conference of Catholic Bishops also gave some similar indications in *New Ecclesial Movements and Associations*.

[107] See *Iuvenescit Ecclesia*, no. 18b, f, g, h.

being based on affective needs to please and thus be recognized by authority or by others. Several criteria indicate the maturity of a community.

The first corresponds to the need to be in *harmony with the Church and obey the Magisterium*.[108] It is not enough to say that the Pope's teaching is followed, but it must be fully honored and not selected according to the interests of the moment. In this way, doctrinal drift and sacramental practices that do not conform to the Church's liturgy are to be avoided.

The second criterion is to be part of the *reality of the local church* in the diocese where one lives. Even if the community legitimately has its own activities, it cannot stand alone, without real integration in the diocesan church. Communion with its pastor as well as submission to his discernment and pastoral projects are signs of ecclesiality.

Another criterion is the *cooperative relationship* that must exist with other Catholic communities and institutions located in the same region. Competition is not conceived. Each community or institution is enriched by the charism of others. Nurturing mistrust and an elitist position fractures the oneness of the Church where vocational unity and diversity are fostered.

A fourth criterion is *respect for the community's statutes* and its rules. Among other aspects, the time for elections and nominations of responsible parties must be respected. Renewing them regularly prevents power being reduced to the same people. In serious cases of non-respect of proper laws, the ecclesiastical authority must intervene.

A fifth criterion is the *equality that exists among the members* of a community. Even if a founder or foundress has a specific mission

---

[108] It means a deep sense of belonging to the Church: "Real communion cannot exist in Movements or in New Communities unless these are integrated within the greater communion of our Holy Mother, the hierarchical Church." Francis, Address (November 22, 2014), no. 3.

in a community, he or she must also submit to its statutes and discipline. Founders and responsible superiors are the first servants of the work that God has entrusted to the Church, not owners of it.

The sixth criterion refers to the *sense of commitment* that people freely assume in a community. They do it in conscience before God. What is promised to Him out of love must be fulfilled according to the rules of the statutes. Breaking the bonds is a serious matter. Still, those who leave the association must be treated with respect and charity.

Finally, the seventh maturity criterion of a community is the *integration of the notions of internal and external forum*. In the *internal forum*, issues of conscience are dealt with, that is, the personal and intimate dimension of each member. The *external forum* concerns the social and behavioral dimension of the subject, every external action carried out concretely.

The confessor exercises his ministry in the *internal forum*, in the depths of a conscience: everything is submitted to the "sacramental seal." The spiritual director also has a duty to keep the secret about everything that is discussed in the spiritual direction dialogues. While spiritual direction is not bound by the sacramental seal like Confession, it is also a privileged conversation that must be kept private. Those who exercise authority in a context of governance are situated in the *external forum*, and the requested obedience concerns what is specified in the statutes (for example formation, missions, responsibilities entrusted to each one, etc.).

By confusing the forums, the risk would be great of using information received in the context of the internal forum to make decisions. Such confusion would create a dependency and submission that would severely hamper people's freedom.

CHAPTER VII

THE
FORMATION

A Transformation

"[May] Christ be formed in you" (Gal. 4:19). St. Paul's words highlight the purpose of formation for every baptized person. This formation is synonymous with transformation. Indeed, training is not simply information, that is, the transmission and acquisition of some notions, even if they are enriching. It is above all a matter of acquiring a form, that of Christ, adopting His way of thinking, feeling, loving, reacting, acting, establishing relationships with others, etc. Fortunately, the Holy Spirit, the first educator of souls, is the main protagonist of this work in the hearts of those who open themselves to His action. It is, after all, a pedagogy of holiness:

> Formation [is] learning to live and think in a Christian way. For example, moral formation does not consist, above all, in defining what is good or bad, but it is the means of conversion, assuming the social consequences of the evangelical demands.[109]

---

[109] Hervé Roullet, *Être laïc et se former dans l'Église d'aujourd'hui* (Bordeaux: D. F. R., 2008), 47 (my translation).

For laypeople, in general, there is no document that establishes a formation program (*ratio formationis*).[110] The transmission of the Faith, offered in an ordinary way in the parish catechetical structure, must be adapted to everyone and to all circumstances of life: children, adolescents, youth, students, adults, the engaged, married couples, professionals, the elderly, the sick, occasional practitioners, the distanced, the reconverted, newcomers, the newly converted and beginners, those disabled in body or spirit, etc. This formation must allow that "the living faith of the faithful [become] manifest and active" (canon 773): it "is ongoing and dynamic."[111]

The *Code of Canon Law* reminds us that the formation of the laity, described in canon 229, has its foundation in the right-duty to the apostolate, explained in canon 225. In fact, canon 229 recalls that it is necessary for the laity to be formed in order to be able to "announce" Christian doctrine and "defend it if necessary" and also to be able to "take their part in exercising the apostolate" (canon 229 §1). It is an extension of canon 217, which formulates for all the faithful the "right to a Christian education" in order to be able to "lead a holy life" (canon 210).

The *Aparecida Document*, no. 280 structures all aspects of Christian Life pertaining to an integral and articulated formation using the following four pillars: human and community; spiritual; intellectual; pastoral and missionary. These elements are the same that structure priestly formation, as indicated in the apostolic exhortation *Pastores dabo vobis* on this matter.[112] These points are

---

[110] Concerning lay formation, see also USCCB, *Co-Workers in the Vineyard of the Lord*, 33–53.

[111] Latin American Episcopal Conference (CELAM), *The Aparecida Document* (Bogotá: CELAM, 2007), no. 279.

[112] John Paul II, Apostolic Exhortation *Pastores dabo vobis* on the Formation of Priests in the Circumstances of the Present Day (March 25, 1992), nos. 42–59.

also included in the formation of consecrated life, perhaps a little less clearly, as can be seen in the directives *Potissimum institutioni*, no. 34 (which evokes the conciliar decree *Optatam totius*, no. 11 on priestly formation).[113]

It is important to ask ourselves what content the movements and new communities offer for the formation of their lay members. A clear formation program could address the four dimensions mentioned by the *Aparecida Document*, no. 280. Following these indications, I propose some general formation themes.

Human and ***community formation*** must lead to molding one's personality according to the life of Christ, including relationships of serene fraternity.

In the human sphere, those in charge of formation in an association must encourage by appropriate means:

✠ self-knowledge, to discover characteristic traits of the personal character and lead to a serene acceptance of its positive and negative aspects;

✠ the ability to meet and dialogue with others, also in the context of a pluralistic society;

✠ affective maturity and sexual balance in a clear identity, with the ability to establish peaceful friendships and sufficient interior freedom, without excessive emotional instability or strong affective dependencies; balanced relationships with any people (men, women, youth, children);

✠ the maturation of conscience, obedient to moral obligations through a well-educated will, with a spirit of sacrifice, which leads to balanced behavior;

[113] Second Vatican Council, Decree *Optatam totius* on Priestly Training (October 28, 1965); Congregation for Institutes of Consecrated Life and Societies of Apostolic Life, Directives *Potissimum institutioni* on Formation in Religious Institutes (February 2, 1990).

✛ the development of personal freedom, just and balanced, which allows openness to others, in the gift of oneself and in service;

✛ growth in the most esteemed virtues: the sense of justice, fidelity to the word given and the commitments made; love of truth, respect for others, balance of judgment and behavior; the ability to make projects (to program) and carry them out; the sense of acceptance and generosity, sharing and sobriety, magnanimity and compassion, prudence and discretion, fidelity and firmness.

In addition, we can include in the field of community formation—understood as referring to the charism of a movement or new community—some additional arguments and points of study:

✛ the spiritual heritage of the community: the history of the founding charism, its spirituality, its aims;

✛ the family spirit, which implies discretion as well as an authentic and healthy self-denial;

✛ fraternal life in community, according to the modalities foreseen: the experience of charity and forgiveness, being an instrument of peace, unity, and communion;

✛ the exercise of authority and the authentic spirit of evangelical obedience required by the statutes; the meaning of dialogue; the distinction and respect of internal and external forum;

✛ zeal for a job or service well done, with fidelity, regularity, and responsibility;

✛ the openness to be educated; acceptance of other members of the association and of people with different cultures and traditions.

When it comes to *spiritual formation*,[114] it must lead to communion with the Lord, through the Word of God and the celebration of the

---

[114] See CNBB, *Mission and Ministries of Lay Christians* (Itaici: Editora Paulinas, 1999), particularly no. 175.

sacraments, in particular the Eucharist. Concretely, this formation should lead the members of the associations to:

- ✠ the love of God and to the exodus from oneself, through active charity towards others;
- ✠ the elaboration and experience of a "life program," according to the spirit of the association;
- ✠ fidelity to spiritual accompaniment, capable of maturing the moral conscience and discerning the signs of God's will;
- ✠ daily conversion through the frequent practice of the examination of conscience and regular Confession;
- ✠ fidelity to the life of prayer, particularly in listening to the Word of God;
- ✠ develop a love for the Liturgy and an awareness of praying with the Church: the rites of the Holy Mass, "being formed by the Eucharist;"[115] the Liturgy of the Hours, etc.;
- ✠ assume a sober and respectful "ecology" of life in the "common home" in which we live; [116]
- ✠ a capacity for spiritual discernment about oneself, the Church, and the realities of the world.

As for **intellectual formation**, it entails deepening the truths revealed by God and the Church's experience of faith. In this way, the danger of an affective spiritualism as a disembodied intellectualism is avoided. Thus, formation must cultivate:

- ✠ the solid familiarity with the "deposit of Faith," contained in the Sacred Scriptures and in the Tradition of the Church;
- ✠ availability in order to seek the truth, enlightening its permanent value to reality and contemporary culture;
- ✠ the ability to expound the Faith according to circumstances, in the light of accumulated knowledge;

---

[115] Francis, Apostolic Letter *Desiderio desideravi* on the Liturgical Formation of the People of God (June 29, 2022), no. 65.

[116] Francis, Encyclical Letter *Laudato si'* on Care for Our Common Home (May 24, 2015), no. 1.

✠ the ability to express calm and objective judgments.

In the intellectual sphere, a structured path can be offered, prepared from the Second Vatican Council documents, the *Catechism of the Catholic Church*, the *Compendium of the Social Doctrine of the Church*, and the rich post-conciliar pontifical Magisterium. Some themes stand out:

✠ introduction to the Sacred Scriptures and Tradition, foundations of the Catholic Faith;

✠ introduction to the life of prayer and the spiritual life, to the great spiritual traditions (Benedictine, Carmelite, Jesuit, etc.);

✠ study of the Liturgy and its rituals, as well as the functions that can be entrusted to laypeople;

✠ moral formation, including current issues: bioethics, sexual and family morals, same-sex unions, etc.;

✠ the Church's social doctrine, including ecological issues;

✠ ecumenism, as well as elements of the Eastern Christian tradition;

✠ interreligious dialogue, demarcating the specificity of Christianity;

✠ the dialogue with the atheists and the indifferent;

✠ the understanding of religious movements (new age, evangelism, etc.);

✠ the participation of laypeople in Church matters;

✠ the media and communication.

These themes and others can also find a very rich study and support for ongoing formation in the documents issued by the various dicasteries of the Roman Curia, but also in the documents produced by the National Episcopal Conference.

It is possible to develop other themes in which laypeople can specialize:

✠ the human sciences (psychology, sociology, etc.);

✠ the sciences of education and communication;

✠ the pedagogy or the way of teaching;

✠ the peculiarity of assistance to certain social groups: the world of education and work, arts and culture in general, science and technology, politics and economics; as well as attention to migrants, the elderly, marginalized, physically or mentally handicapped, chemically dependent, etc.

Finally, ***pastoral*** and ***missionary formation*** must prepare missionaries to be capable of dialogue, animated by the desire and interior need to announce salvation to everyone. The apostolates of the movements and new communities are concrete places of self-giving and expressions of Christ's love for men. In this context, the following must be developed:

✠ communion and collaboration with other ecclesial realities;

✠ the capacity for progressive insertion in the pastoral praxis of the association itself, but also that of the diocese and parish;

✠ the capacity for discernment, initiative, programming, animation, and leadership;

✠ proximity to people, their problems and questions, attention to the poor and sick.

The mission of formation seems immense and daunting. As a result, some individuals might believe that they must excel in every subject matter. But this is far from the truth. First, the aim of formation should be for the members of the movement or new community to acquire a sufficient basis so that, as Christians and citizens, they can dialogue with society. Some members will be able to receive a more specialized formation, by obtaining academic degrees in order to better serve the Church's mission through their own charism.

CHAPTER VIII

LITURGY

Divine Worship and the Service of Men

---

1. Active Participation, Internal and External

In 2007 the USCCB published *Sing to the Lord: Music in Divine Worship*, a guide to shed light on the role and ministry of liturgical music. This relevant document remains largely unknown. However, it should inspire celebrations in the new associations. The latter, in turn, can be a valuable instrument of education in the Faith, seeking to make the liturgical celebration a deed of God and a service to men.

The episcopal document, carefully drafted and richly adorned with information, offers clues for liturgical celebrations that are valid for ecclesial movements and new communities. Among other things, it states that "the Liturgy calls for significant periods of silent reflection. Silence need not always be filled."[117] In fact, "music arises out of silence and returns to silence,"[118] and in a culture of noise it "must also be counter-cultural."[119]

---

[117] *Sing to the Lord: Music in Divine Worship* (Washington, DC: USCCB Publishing, 2007), no. 91.
[118] Ibid., no. 118.
[119] Ibid., no. 12.

From this document, aspects to be developed with intelligence and care can be highlighted:

✠ use musical instruments not only to accompany the singing, but also to perform a prelude, an interlude, or a postlude, and thus provide a climate of interiorization: "There are also times when the organ or other instruments may be played alone, such as a prelude before the Mass, an instrumental piece during the Preparation of the Gifts, a recessional if there is no closing song, or a postlude following a closing song."[120]

✠ avoid too much change of repertoire, looking for novelty or successful songs: without excluding a variety of new songs, "familiarity with a stable repertoire of liturgical songs rich in theological content can deepen the faith of the community through repetition and memorization."[121]

✠ watch over an individualistic search for God based on mere feelings, without the depth and breadth of Christian commitment, or without communion with the brothers:[122] indeed music "is capable of expressing a dimension of meaning and

[120] Ibid., no. 44.

[121] Ibid., no. 27.

[122] It is useful to recall the Letter on Some Aspects of Christian Meditation from the Congregation for the Doctrine of the Faith (October 15, 1989). A certain intimate and sentimental religiosity can lead one to believe that certain sensations are "authentic consolations of the Holy Spirit," to the point of even "giving them a symbolic significance typical of the mystical experience, when the moral condition of the person concerned does not correspond to such an experience, [in] a kind of mental schizophrenia" (no. 28). Let us also remember that the Messalians, "false fourth-century charismatics [who] identified the grace of the Holy Spirit with the psychological experience of his presence in the soul" (no. 9). Pope Francis states: "Jesus ... is not found by those who seek miracles, ... by those who seek new sensations, intimate experiences, strange things; those who seek a faith made up of power and external signs. No, they will not find him.... Jesus asks you to accept him in the daily reality that you live; in the Church of today, as it is; in those who are close to you every day; in the reality of those in need, in the problems of your family.... He is there." *Angelus* (January 30, 2022).

feeling that words alone cannot convey. While this dimension of an individual musical composition is often difficult to describe, its affective power should be carefully considered along with its textual component."[123]

In the still recent past, some liturgical options that led to certain abusive celebrations undoubtedly started out in good faith, seeking to incorporate faithful members of the laity into those celebrations. For instance, "active participation" desired by the conciliar constitution *Sacrosanctum Concilium* is, this text adds, both internal and external.[124] In fact, how can these two aspects of participation be dissociated since they characterize two sides of the same reality? There can be no opposition between them, since every human act is an interior act and an exterior act:[125] they constitute a single reality, as the body and soul constitute a single person.

As Cardinal Joseph Ratzinger asked: "But cannot this 'participation' also include receptivity on the part of the spirit and the senses? Is there really nothing 'active' in perceiving, receiving, and being inwardly moved? This is surely a diminution of man, a reduction to what can be expressed in speech.... In questioning this approach, we are not, of course, opposing the efforts being made to encourage the whole congregation to sing, nor are we against 'utility music' in itself. But what we must oppose is the exclusivity which insists on *that* music alone and which is justified neither by the Council nor by pastoral necessity."[126]

Active participation sometimes took on a purely external and superficial meaning, reducing itself to the idea that people should

---

[123] *Sing to the Lord*, no. 124.

[124] See Second Vatican Council, Constitution *Sacrosanctum Concilium* on the Sacred Liturgy (December 4, 1963), no. 19.

[125] See St. Thomas Aquinas, *Summa Theologica* Ia–IIae, q. 18, art. 6.

[126] Joseph Ratzinger, *The Ratzinger Report: An Exclusive Interview on the State of the Church* (San Francisco, CA: Ignatius Press, 1985), 128–129.

be manifestly active in the Liturgy.[127] *Active participation* then became exclusively about external, tangible activities (speeches, words, songs, homilies, readings, movements, gestures, etc.). To respond to this anxiety, a new liturgical concept of freedom and creativity has been created.[128]

> The grandeur of the liturgy does not rest upon the fact that it offers an interesting entertainment, but in rendering tangible the Totally Other, whom we are not capable of summoning. He comes because He wills. [...] Men experiment with it in lively fashion, and find themselves deceived, when the mystery is transformed into distraction, when the chief actor in the liturgy is not the Living God but the priest or the liturgical director.[129]

In this way, the integral thought of the Council was excluded, which also dealt with the need for deep and interior participation, even silent, allowing the Lord to be listened to.[130]

It does not seem vain to retranslate what Joseph Ratzinger said about a certain conception of the Liturgy:

> The liturgy is not a show, a spectacle, requiring brilliant producers and talented actors. The life of the liturgy does not consist in "pleasant" surprises and attractive "ideas" but in solemn repetitions. It cannot be an expression of what is current and transitory, for it expresses the mystery of the Holy. Many people have felt and said that liturgy must be "made" by the whole community if it is really to belong to them. Such an attitude has led to the "success"

---

[127] See Joseph Ratzinger, *The Spirit of the Liturgy* (San Francisco, CA: Ignatius Press, 2000), 185–191.

[128] See Joseph Ratzinger, *The Feast of Faith: Approaches to a Theology of the Liturgy* (San Francisco, CA: Ignatius Press, 1986), 61.

[129] Joseph Ratzinger, Address to the Chilean Bishops (July 13, 1988).

[130] See Joseph Ratzinger, *The Ratzinger Report*, 127.

of the liturgy being measured by its effect at the level of spectacle and entertainment. It is to lose sight of what is *distinctive* to the liturgy, which does not come from what *we do* but from the fact that something is *taking place* here that all of us together cannot "make." In the liturgy there is a power, an energy at work which not even the Church as a whole can generate: what it manifests is the Wholly Other, coming to us through the community (which is hence not sovereign but servant, purely instrumental). Liturgy, for the Catholic, is his common homeland, the source of his identity. And another reason why it must be something "given" and "constant" is that, by means of the ritual, it manifests the holiness of God. The revolt against what has been described as "the old rubricist rigidity," which was accused of stifling "creativity," has in fact made the liturgy into a do-it-yourself patchwork and trivialized it, adapting it to our mediocrity.[131]

In addition to what has been said, it is worth retaining other elements of the USCCB document: "The importance of the priest's participation in the Liturgy, especially by singing, cannot be overemphasized. The priest sings the presidential prayers and dialogues of the Liturgy according to his capabilities,"[132] as well as the Preface, Anamnesis, and Doxology, as the centuries-old tradition proposes.[133] Even if Gregorian chant and sacred polyphony disappeared almost completely from our assemblies, "the Second Vatican Council directed that the faithful be able to sing parts of the Ordinary of the Mass together in Latin.... Every effort in this regard is laudable and highly encouraged."[134] Therefore, Gregorian

[131] Ibid., 126–127.
[132] *Sing to the Lord*, no. 19.
[133] See also Congregation of Sacred Rites, Instruction *Musicam Sacram* on Music in the Liturgy (March 5, 1967), 29–31.
[134] *Sing to the Lord*, no. 74.

chant is a "musical treasure" of the Church[135] and has a "pride of place" in the Liturgy.[136]

On the topic of Gregorian chant, the USCCB text affirms that the faithful "should be able to sing these parts of the Mass proper to them, at least according to the simpler melodies,"[137] especially "for generally unrehearsed community singing."[138] In some communities, simple (syllabic) Gregorian chants could be performed by the assembly, such as: the *Kyrie, Sanctus, Agnus Dei.*[139] Naturally, difficult and more elaborate (melismatic) songs could be performed only by the *Schola Cantorum*, or by a soloist, in moments of interiorization and listening, or in "alternation, especially the *Gloria*, the Creed, and the three processional songs: the Entrance, the Preparation of the Gifts, and Communion."[140] Finally, "every attempt should be made to sing the acclamations [Gospel Acclamation, Memorial Acclamation, and the Great Amen] and dialogues."[141]

All of this must not remain in complaint but constitute a real challenge and encouragement for ecclesial movements and new

---

[135] "Instead many liturgists have thrust this treasure aside, calling it 'esoteric' and treating it slightingly in the name of an 'intelligibility for all and at every moment, which ought to characterize the post-conciliar liturgy.' [One looks] only [to] have 'utility music,' songs, easy melodies, catchy tunes." Joseph Ratzinger, *The Ratzinger Report*, 127–128. Certainly, "to rely only on the music of a single genre or style for the celebration of the Liturgy is to diminish the breadth and depth of our liturgical heritage and to risk the exclusion of the legitimate contributions of particular cultures and composers." Committee on Divine Worship of the United States Conference of Catholic Bishops, *Stewards of the Tradition: Fifty Years After "Sacrosanctum Concilium"* (n.p.: USCCB, September 2013), no. 3.

[136] *Sing to the Lord*, no. 73.

[137] Ibid., no. 61.

[138] Ibid., no. 28.

[139] See ibid., no. 75.

[140] Ibid., no. 29.

[141] Ibid., no. 116.

communities, which make the Liturgy a constitutive element of their celebrations. Thus, an authentic encounter with God will strengthen all the Lord's disciples in their missionary vocation: "How can we not dream of a Church which reflects and echoes the harmony of voices and song in her daily life!"[142]

2. The Liturgy of the Hours

The varied expressions of divine worship play an important role in the life of different associations. Some have regular meetings, even daily, for personal and community prayer. It is interesting to underline how the Liturgy of the Hours has been valued.

Without a doubt, the Liturgy of the Hours is an excellent means of guaranteeing the regularity of divine praise in response to the invitation of the Lord who said, "Pray always" (Luke 18:1). In addition to the daily Holy Mass, Lauds and Vespers are particularly honored in the daily organization of prayer. As the Council recalled, because they are related to the death and Resurrection of Christ, "by the venerable tradition of the universal Church, Lauds as morning prayer and Vespers as evening prayer are the two hinges on which the daily office turns; hence they are to be considered as the chief hours and are to be celebrated as such."[143]

Furthermore, the Constitution *Sacrosanctum Concilium*, no. 100 says: "The laity, too, are encouraged to recite the divine office, either with the priests, or among themselves, or even individually." In this context, it should be noted that "the sung celebration of the divine office is more in keeping with the nature of this prayer and a mark of both higher solemnity and closer union of hearts in offering praise to God.... Therefore, the singing of the office is

---

[142] Francis, Address at Vespers in Assunción, Paraguay (July 11, 2015).
[143] *Sacrosanctum Concilium*, 89a.

earnestly recommended to those who carry out the office in choir or in common."[144]

Pope Paul VI also affirms in the apostolic constitution *Laudis Canticum*: "The Liturgy of the Hours ... is offered to all the faithful, even to those who are not bound by law to recite it."[145] In fact, "nor is the Church's praise to be considered either by origin or by nature the exclusive possession of clerics and monks but the property of the whole Christian community."[146] Thus, "their public or communal celebration should be encouraged, especially in the case of those who live in community."[147]

The General Instruction on the Liturgy of the Hours already said in number 27:

> Lay groups gathering for prayer, apostolic work, or any other reason are encouraged to [celebrate] part of the liturgy of the hours. The laity must learn above all how in the liturgy they are adoring God the Father in spirit and in truth; they should bear in mind that through public worship and prayer they reach all humanity and can contribute significantly to the salvation of the whole world. Finally, it is of great advantage for the family, the domestic sanctuary of the Church, not only to pray together to God but also to celebrate some parts of the liturgy of the hours as occasion offers, in order to enter more deeply into the life of the Church.

---

[144] Congregation for Divine Worship, General Instruction on the Liturgy of the Hours (February 2, 1971), no. 268.

[145] Paul VI, Apostolic Constitution *Laudis canticum* Promulgating the Divine Office as Revised in Accordance with the Decree of the Second Ecumenical Council of the Vatican (November 1, 1970), no. 8.

[146] General Instruction on the Liturgy of the Hours, no. 270.

[147] Ibid., no. 40.

The Synod of Bishops on the Word of God, held in 2008, "asked that this prayer become more widespread among the People of God, particularly the recitation of Morning Prayer and Evening Prayer."[148]

Since Holy Mass is the culmination of the Church's life and holiness and of every ecclesial association, the Liturgy of the Hours then becomes the necessary continuation of the Eucharist.[149] The Liturgy of the Hours is an act of thanksgiving for God's creative and salvific work.

The prayer of the Hours allows us to truly live the "Eucharistic form of Christian life" that Benedict XVI spoke of in the apostolic exhortation *Sacramentum Caritatis*.[150] We continue offering ourselves to God as we do in each Eucharist. In this way, "taking part in the liturgy of the hours [we] have access to holiness of the richest kind through the life-giving word of God, which in this liturgy receives great emphasis."[151]

---

[148] Benedict XVI, Apostolic Exhortation *Verbum Domini* on the Word of God in the Life and Mission of the Church (September 30, 2010), no. 62.

[149] See *Laudis canticum*, no. 2.

[150] Benedict XVI, Apostolic Exhortation *Sacramentum Caritatis* on the Eucharist as the Source and Summit of the Church's Life and Mission (February 22, 2007), no. 76.

[151] General Instruction on the Liturgy of the Hours, no. 14.

CHAPTER IX

RELATION TO
THE LOCAL CHURCH

Dynamism of Communion[152]

—————•———≈•≈———•—————

1. Difficulties Encountered

THE STUDY OF THE National Conference of Bishops of Brazil *Lay Christians in Church and Society* stated that movements and new communities "are born out of a desire to serve the Church, in carrying out its mission of announcing Jesus Christ and building God's Kingdom." And it further noted: "Throughout history, many of these forms of organization of the laity ... had an initial relationship with the Church marked by tensions, difficulties and sufferings, until they found a form of recognition."[153]

It should be remembered that every parish will always have a fundamental and irreplaceable role as the first incarnation of the Gospel where the Word of God is announced and the Christian life is nourished by the sacraments and service.[154] Associations

---

[152] A part of this chapter is the personal translation of Arturo Cattaneo, "The Relationship between the Parish and Ecclesial Movements," interview on *ZENIT*, December 17, 2004; English version January 10, 2005.

[153] CNBB, *Lay Christians*, no. 207.

[154] Some sacraments, such as Baptism and Matrimony, can only be received within the parish (without a dispensation). Indeed, the parish "remains an indispensable organism of primary importance in the

"cannot place themselves on the same level as parish communities as possible alternatives"[155] and cannot constitute themselves as a "parallel church,"[156] especially because the ecclesiastical authorities that approve their statutes have a duty to monitor their actions. But it is also obvious that the parish is not the only way in which the Church responds to the needs of evangelization,[157] nor does its activity exclude other forms of Christian life:[158] "The parish has no right to exclude or deny the existence of movements and associations that express the manifold grace of God."[159]

Any new reality faces the danger of ignoring the local church's experiences and the Spirit working through her. At the same time, the local church can be close-minded when she does not allow herself to be fertilized by these new charisms. Instead, she simply wants to use some individuals without really accepting what is proper to them. In fact, in such a situation, it is not easy for associations to preserve their specificity without diluting their identity, especially

---

visible structure of the Church." Congregation for the Clergy, Instruction *The Pastoral Conversion of the Parish Community in the Service of the Evangelizing Mission of the Church* (July 20, 2020), no. 12.

[155] CNBB, *Community of Communities: A New Parish* (São Paulo: Editora Paulinas, 2014), 235.

[156] See *Iuvenescit Ecclesia*, no. 23.

[157] See *Pastoral Conversion of the Parish Community*, no. 29.

[158] A parish, especially the biggest, might become a "community of communities." Apostolic Exhortation *Ecclesia in America* on the Encounter with the Living Jesus Christ: The Way to Conversion, Communion, and Solidarity in America (January 22, 1999), no. 41.

[159] CNBB, *Community of Communities*, 235. Also, because the current parish model is no longer "the primary gathering and social center, as in former days" and "no longer adequately corresponds to the many expectations of the faithful" (*Pastoral Conversion of the Parish Community*, nos. 14, 16), parishes "are not the only ways of gathering people into community and equipping them for mission. Movements can exist within parishes and alongside of parishes." H. Richard McCord, *Ecclesial Movements as Agents of a New Evangelization*, Resource for Catechetical Sunday (Washington, DC: USCCB, 2012), 4.

when serving a pastoral activity perhaps already lacking in spirit, when they could bring a new and lively approach.

Movement members, remaining faithful to their charism, must try to creatively insert this charism into the local church's life. It is worth remembering the spirit of service that the members of the associations will willingly give to the initiatives of the bishop and parish priest, in accordance with the characteristics of their own charism. But this does not necessarily mean that they should be present, as representatives of the movement, in diocesan or parish bodies. In fact, the first area of ecclesial action proper to the lay faithful is, of course, the family, then social, professional, political, cultural, sporting, etc.

2. Communion: Unity and Plurality

Sometimes one's concept of communion is inaccurate. Monsignor M. Delgado Galindo, under-secretary of the former Pontifical Council for the Laity, affirms that "if *insertion* meant the integration or adaptation within the particular Churches of members of ecclesial movements …, such an expression would not do justice to these faithful, who already live their own faith and seek to work with a sense of communion…. The term *insertion* would be even less appropriate if with it one wished to indicate the inclusion of charisms in particular Churches … as if such charisms were something accessory or secondary to be incorporated into a whole already complete."[160]

The then Cardinal Joseph Ratzinger, on the occasion of the first World Congress organized by the Pontifical Council for the Laity on ecclesial movements and new communities, also stated in his speech of May 27, 1998:

[160] Miguel Delgado Galindo, *Movimenti ecclesiali, ministero petrino e apostolicità della Chiesa* (Rome: VivereIn, 2007), 36–37 (my translation).

The bishops must be reminded that they must avoid any uniformity of pastoral organizations and programs.... [It] could render the Churches impervious to the action of the Holy Spirit.... Not everything should be fitted into the straightjacket of a single uniform organization.... Above all, a concept of *communio*, in which the highest pastoral value is attached to the avoidance of conflict [in the name of an illusory internal peace], should be rejected.... What, in the last analysis, needs to be established is not a blasé attitude of intellectual superiority that immediately brands the zeal of those seized by the Holy Spirit and their uninhibited faith with the anathema of fundamentalism, and only authorizes a faith in which the ifs and buts are more important than the substance of what is believed. In the last analysis everyone must let himself be measured by the unity of the one Church.[161]

Thus, "ecclesial movements must, according to their own charism and possibility, collaborate with the pastoral projects carried out in the particular church. This does not mean that all members of the particular church must work in the same field, at the same time, and in the same way. In fact, the faithful can also build the Church by living a certain charism. Therefore, the plurality of ministries, charisms, and forms of life in no way affects the unity of the particular Church; on the contrary, it enriches it."[162]

---

[161] Joseph Ratzinger, "The Ecclesial Movements: A Theological Reflection on Their Place in the Church," in *Movements in the Church: Proceedings of the World Congress of the Ecclesial Movements, Rome, 27–29 May, 1998*, ed. Pontifical Council for the Laity (Vatican City: Pontificium Consilium pro Laicis, 1999), 50–51.

[162] Delgado Galindo, *Movimenti ecclesiali*, 39 (my translation).

3. EFFECTIVE COMMUNION

How to overcome possible tensions in ecclesial relations?[163]

Recently Pope Francis insisted that "it will prove beneficial [for the movements] not to lose contact with the rich reality of the local parish and to participate readily in the overall pastoral activity of the particular Church. This kind of integration will prevent them from concentrating only on part of the Gospel or the Church, or becoming nomads without roots."[164] It is impossible to conceive that an ecclesial institution would be indifferent to a diocese's pastoral concerns.

This integration, as Cardinal Marc Ouellet states, "implies a pastoral conversion that promotes as a priority the establishment of good personal or institutional contact.... [Sometimes] the pastoral relationship of mutual listening is not established ... because it is impeded by an image of rejection."[165] To integrate associations more visibly in the particular church as desired by *Evangelii gaudium*, "each one will find the way to do so respecting his own charism and that of others, happy to contribute to the missionary expansion of the

---

[163] "Those who are called to a service of discernment and guidance should not claim to dominate charisms but rather to guard against the danger of suffocating them (cf. 1 Thes 5:19–21), resisting the temptation to standardize what the Holy Spirit desired to be multi-form to contribute to building and extending the one Body of Christ, which the same Spirit renders firm in unity.... The Bishop must examine the charisms and test them, to recognize and appreciate what is good, true and beautiful, what contributes to the increase of holiness, of both individuals and communities.... Difficulties or misunderstanding on specific questions do not authorize their closure." Benedict XVI, Address (May 17, 2008).

[164] *Evangelii gaudium*, no. 29.

[165] Marc Ouellet, "Evangelizing by Attraction: The People of God as a People of Joy; The Permanent Fecundity of the Charisms Reveals Itself in Communion and in Mission" (conference at the Congress of Ecclesial Movements and New Communities, Rome, November 20, 2014; my translation).

Church. Obviously, this orientation of the Pope calls the particular Church to a greater openness to the particular charisms of laypeople or consecrated persons who are an integral, co-essential part of the mission of the People of God.... The mission of the particular Church consists in giving a missionary witness of communion."[166]

Pope John Paul II also affirmed that these new associations must "share their charismatic riches with humility and generosity within the communion and mission of the local Churches."[167] At the same time, he declared: "I therefore recommend that they be spread."[168] Therefore, "the insertion of a charismatic reality in a particular Church consists in spreading this charism in a spirit of humility."[169]

And this spirit of humility is manifested by esteeming the realities of service and collaboration within a particular Church, especially concerning the faithful who live according to other charisms or ecclesial commitments.[170] In this context, communion with the diocesan bishop is essential: "There remains a need, however, to ensure that these associations actively participate in the Church's overall pastoral efforts,"[171] in a profound communion "not only in faith but in action."[172]

It is therefore necessary to respect the freedom of association of the faithful.[173] This freedom finds its intrinsic limit in the obligation

---

[166] Ibid. Really, "the local Churches and movements are not in opposition to one another, but constitute the living structure of the Church." Benedict XVI, Address to the German Bishops (August 21, 2005).

[167] John Paul II, Message to the Participants in the Seminar on Ecclesial Movements and New Communities, June 18, 1999, no. 3.

[168] John Paul II, Encyclical Letter *Redemptoris missio* on the Permanent Validity of the Church's Missionary Mandate (December 7, 1990), no. 72.

[169] Delgado Galindo, *Movimenti ecclesiali*, 40.

[170] See *Christifideles laici*, no. 30.

[171] *Evangelii gaudium*, no. 105.

[172] *The Aparecida Document*, no. 313.

[173] See Second Vatican Council, Decree *Apostolicam actuositatem* on the Apostolate of the Laity (November 18, 1965), no. 18; canon 215.

to observe communion with the Church and, therefore, her unity (see canon 209). In fact, freedom and unity are not in opposition, as affirming the first does not mean denying the second. These are two simultaneous and harmonious requirements of ecclesial communion. Lack of freedom would not benefit the unity; on the contrary, it would cause disintegration.

Each association has its own charism and its members are called to live it in family, social, professional, political, cultural, sporting, etc. Without a doubt, due to their creative dynamism, "the movements and new communities are an opportunity for many people who are distant to have an experience of a living encounter with Jesus Christ."[174] Perhaps radiating this presence is the movements' main contribution to the particular church. New associations have some differing characteristics from the parish: one of them is to transcend the parochial and, at times, diocesan context.[175] Thus, the movements and new communities help to form mature Christian personalities, aware of their baptismal identity, of their own vocation and mission in the Church and in the world, able, moreover, to offer a significant witness of Christian life: "Your Movements witness the joy of the faith and the beauty of being Christian."[176]

---

[174] *The Aparecida Document*, no. 312.

[175] Some associations are "supra-diocesan," but "when they possess a supra-diocesan character, [they] must not consider themselves as completely autonomous from the particular Church; rather, they should enrich and serve her precisely through that particularity which is shared beyond the confines of a single diocese." *Iuvenescit Ecclesia*, no. 21.

[176] Benedict XVI, Address to the Bishop-Friends of the Focolare Movement and the Sant'Egidio Community (February 8, 2007).

CHAPTER X

"ECCLESIAL FAMILIES"

New Forms of Consecrated Life (Canon 605)[177]

———— ·——— ⌇•⌇ ——·————

1. Canonical Considerations about the New Associations

The statutes of various associations evoke the *charism of communion*. John Paul II profoundly and meaningfully describes the principle of communion, which is to be lived in specific ways:

> We need *to promote a spirituality of communion*, making it the guiding principle of education wherever individuals and Christians are formed, wherever ministers of the altar, consecrated persons, and pastoral workers are trained, wherever families and communities are being built up. A spirituality of communion indicates above all the heart's contemplation of the mystery of the Trinity dwelling in us, and whose light we must also be able to see shining on the face of the brothers and sisters around

---

[177] I have translated into French an unpublished Italian text on this subject: Leonello Leidi, "Connaître et discerner les nouvelles formes de consécration." *Vies consacrées* 87 (2015): 30–43.

us. A spirituality of communion also means an ability to think of our brothers and sisters in faith within the profound unity of the Mystical Body, and therefore as "those who are a part of me." This makes us able to share their joys and sufferings, to sense their desires and attend to their needs, to offer them deep and genuine friendship. A spirituality of communion implies also the ability to see what is positive in others, to welcome it and prize it as a gift from God: not only as a gift for the brother or sister who has received it directly, but also as a "gift for me." A spirituality of communion means, finally, to know how to "make room" for our brothers and sisters, bearing "each other's burdens" (Gal 6:2) and resisting the selfish temptations which constantly beset us and provoke competition, careerism, distrust and jealousy. Let us have no illusions: unless we follow this spiritual path, external structures of communion will serve very little purpose. They would become mechanisms without a soul, "masks" of communion rather than its means of expression and growth.[178]

Some associations address a charism's *communion of states of life.* These consist of some clerics and, above all, laypeople, some of whom take the evangelical counsels through vows or other private ties. These do not change their state of life, as they are not part of an institute of consecrated life. In this way, evoking the communion of states of life is not accurate, since the paradigmatic order of the consecrated life recognized as such by the Church is lacking.

Some new associations seek to gain recognition for the consecrated life. John Paul II was quite clear when he said in *Vita consecrata*, no. 62 that ecclesial movements and new communities cannot be considered a "new form of consecrated life," according to canon

---

[178] John Paul II, Apostolic Letter *Novo millenio ineunte* at the Close of the Great Jubilee of the Year 2000 (January 6, 2001), 43.

605. The presence of married couples poses the greatest challenge for these associations. In order to have "consecrated life," besides the Church's approval, it is necessary to commit to perfect or perpetual continence in celibacy. It is clear, therefore, that the consecrated life is not reconcilable with the Sacrament of Marriage.

However, since recognition of consecrated life is not the responsibility of the Dicastery for Laity, Family, and Life, certain new associations have recourse to the Dicastery for Institutes of Consecrated Life and Societies of Apostolic Life. This Dicastery, approving an institute of consecrated life within an association of the faithful (movement or new community), would give canonical existence to consecrated life. In this case, belonging to the institute is also belonging to the movement or community. In reality, there would be two distinct canonical entities, under the responsibility of two different Dicasteries, and a dual membership of the consecrated members: to the institute and to the movement.

In this case, there exists the communion of states of life. But let us emphasize the double belonging of consecrated persons to different canonical institutions. Still, the need for fraternal communion can be experienced in different ways: the familial spirit, times of formation and meetings, occasional common prayer, as well as the investment of each one in apostolic activities. All—laypeople, clerics, and consecrated persons—would be linked by the same charism and at the service of the common fraternal work.

2. ECCLESIAL FAMILIES OF CONSECRATED LIFE

A new way of living the communion of states of life is the adoption of a framework established by the Congregation for Institutes of Consecrated Life and Societies of Apostolic Life in 2002.[179]

---

[179] A copy of the outline was given to us by the Dicastery.

The new entity—which is designated as an "ecclesial family of consecrated life"[180]—provides for a single canonical structure, composed of two main branches of consecrated members *pleno iure*—distinctly the male branch and the female branch—and a branch of lay associates. Each branch has its own general superior or moderator, whose function is to govern the particular structure to which he belongs.

Above the entire community there is a *president*, a consecrated man or woman, whose function is to maintain communion among all the members as well as to coordinate, with his or her own authority, the spiritual and apostolic action common to the three branches of the single entity. This structure is intended for all associations that wish to receive effective canonical approval for consecrated life—whose competence is exclusive to the Dicastery for Institutes of Consecrated Life and Societies of Apostolic Life—but who do not conveniently enter into the existing structures provided for in the *Code of Canon Law* of 1983: religious institutes, secular institutes, societies of apostolic life (when evangelical counsels are assumed), hermits and virgins, whether alone or in association.

2.1 *New Forms of Consecrated Life*[181]

The Apostolic Constitution on the Roman Curia *Praedicate Evangelium* recalls that the Dicastery for Institutes of Consecrated Life

---

[180] This structure does not yet have a clearly defined terminology: a *new form of consecrated life*, a *new form of consecration*, a *new community*, a *new foundation*, a *new form of evangelical life*. I will use the expression *ecclesial family of consecrated life* that the Holy See gave for the first time to the Community of the Beatitudes on December 8, 2020: the term *family* seems to emphasize unity in the communion of diversity (lay, consecrated, clergy).

[181] About the supposed novelty of this form, I advise: Vincenzo Bertolone, "Nuove comunità e vita consacrata," in *Nuove forme di vita consacrata*, ed. R. Fusco and G. Rocca (Rome: Urbaniana University Press, 2010), 39–53; Gianfranco Ghirlanda, "Nuove forme di vita

and Societies of Apostolic Life is responsible "for approving and regulating forms of consecrated life that are new with respect to those already recognized by law." [182] The novelty of these "new forms" does not consist of the inclusion of a new "essential element,"[183] as one can read in the document below. The Holy Spirit preserves the basic unity and essence of consecrated life.

These new types of institutes of consecrated life need regulations different from those that already exist in canon law, which are the following: religious institutes; secular institutes; societies of apostolic life that assume the evangelical counsels; hermit life (solitary or associated); consecrated virginity and consecrated widows (individual or associated). Indeed, the new forms "display new characteristics compared to those of traditional Foundations" (*Vita consecrata*, no. 62).

What follows below is a translation from the original Italian of the *Criteria for the Approval of New Forms of Consecrated Life*,[184] by the Congregation for Institutes of Consecrated Life and Societies of

---

consacrata in relazione al can. 605," in *Nuove forme di vita consacrata*, 55–71; Velasio De Paolis, "Le nuove forme di vita consacrata," in *Nuove forme di vita consacrata*, 19–38; Jesús Torres, "Criteri di approvazione delle nuove comunità: La prassi della Congregazione per gli Istituti di Vita Consacrata e le Società di Vita Apostolica," in *Nuove forme di vita consacrata*, 219–225.

[182] Francis, Apostolic Constitution *Praedicate Evangelium* on the Roman Curia and Its Service to the Church in the World (March 19, 2022), 122 §3.

[183] In this sense, John Paul II states: "In this newness however the Spirit does not contradict himself. Proof of this is the fact that the new forms of consecrated life have not supplanted the earlier ones. Amid such wide variety the underlying unity has been successfully preserved, thanks to the one call to follow Jesus—chaste, poor and obedient—in the pursuit of perfect charity. This call, which is found in all the existing forms of consecrated life, must also mark those which present themselves as new." *Vita consecrata*, no. 12.

[184] Giancarlo Rocca, "Le nuove comunità," *Quaderni di diritto ecclesiale* 5 (1992): 171–172, n. 25.

Apostolic Life, approved on January 26, 1990. Filled with clarity, especially considering the scheme of statutes also given here in its entirety, this document needs no explanation.

1. It is a question of a "form of consecrated life" when it includes the essential elements from canons 573–605, that is: a) profession of the evangelical counsels with sacred bonds assumed according to common and proper law; b) stability of life; c) dedication, with a new and special title, to the honor of God, to the edification of the Church, and to the salvation of the world; d) fraternal life, proper to each institute; e) internal superiors, endowed with authority according to common and proper law; f) just autonomy of life, especially of government; g) a fundamental code, approved by the competent ecclesiastical authority; h) canonical erection established by the competent ecclesiastical authority.

2. It is a question of a "new form of consecrated life" when it does not easily fall under any of the other forms already established: religious institutes, secular institutes, societies of apostolic life that assume the evangelical counsels, eremitic life (solitary or associated), or consecrated virginity (individual or associated).

3. Institutes may include different types of people: clerics and laypeople (men and women) bound by a common direction towards the spiritual goal of the institute. When these institutes contain all the elements described above in no. 1, but their complex organization prevents them from being included in one of the categories indicated above in no. 2, then these institutes can be recognized as institutes with a "new form of consecrated life."

4. Regarding "new forms of consecrated life" that also include a clerical branch, it is not necessary for such institutes to be recognized as "clerical"; it is enough that the clerics incardinated in the institute are under the authority of a member who is a priest with the necessary faculties, regardless of whether or not he is also president of the institute.

5. Regarding the number of members (of each branch), the criteria given for institutes of consecrated life and for societies of apostolic life are to be followed.

6. Given the uniqueness of "new forms of consecrated life," it would be more appropriate, subject to the examination and approval of the Dicastery, to authorize the diocesan bishop to erect an institute of diocesan right as a new form of consecrated life and approve its constitutions, *ad experimentum et ad nutum Sanctae Sedis* [on an experimental basis and at the disposition of the Holy See], without time limits, to be submitted for approval by the Holy See when the proposed institute has demonstrated its validity and ecclesial viability. Both the bishop who erects the institute and the general moderator must report annually (or biennially) to the Holy See on the state of the institute, in order to be able to follow the progress of these "new forms," the approval of which is reserved only to the Holy See.

2.2 AN OUTLINE FOR STATUTES

The 2002 outline contains a plan of statutes common to two branches of consecrated persons. The lay branch can draw inspiration from this outline for drafting its own statutes, making necessary adaptations and excluding the profession of vows for married persons. The outline's main points from the Congregation for Institutes of Consecrated Life and Societies of Apostolic Life are as follows in my translation from the original French.

> **General outline concerning the constitutions of an association of the faithful formed of two main branches (single men and single women) with a view towards being erected as an institute of consecrated life.**
>
> The purpose of this document is to indicate the essential material which the Fundamental Code of the Association must deal with, in accordance with the *Code of Canon Law*. The contents of the indicated canons are

to be included in the Constitutions "by analogy," with adaptations for its particular case, in addition to other general elements.

In the Constitutions the spiritual and juridical elements must be well harmonized, but the norms must not be multiplied unnecessarily (see canon 587 §3). Terms normally used for religious institutes should be avoided as much as possible.

All other norms, established or approved by the competent authority of the Association, must be brought together in other Codes (Directory, Customs, etc.) and may be revised and adapted according to the requirements of place and time (see canon 587 §4).

Chapter I: Nature and Purpose of the Association

Begin with an article that states that the Association is made up of two main branches: a) celibate consecrated men (clerics and laity); b) celibate consecrated women. Members of these two branches take the private vows of chastity, poverty, and obedience.

Married couples can be part of the Association, but only as "associate members," according to their own Statutes indicating their organization and their relationship with the Association.

The two main branches have a separate juridical structure, with a president who has authority over the whole Association, elected in the General Assembly. The president is assisted by his council, composed of the general superiors and the respective councils of the two branches.

Define the charism of the Association and indicate the works of apostolate.

Chapter II: Consecration with Vows of Chastity, Poverty, and Obedience

Consecration through private vows; chastity (canon 599); poverty (canon 600); obedience (canon 601; 590 §2); formula of temporary and perpetual vows.

Chapter III: Life with God

The spirit of prayer; daily participation, if possible, in the Eucharist (canon 663 §2); celebration of the Liturgy of the Hours; personal prayer; monthly recollection and annual spiritual retreat; frequent participation in the Sacrament of Reconciliation; other exercises of piety, such as prayers for sick members, for deceased members, and others.

Chapter IV: Fraternal Life

Chapter V: The Apostolic Life

Chapter VI: Integration and Formation Stages

A. *General Principles regarding Formation*

B. *Stages of Formation*

Probationary period; temporary private vows: admission to temporary vows by the general superior, with the consent of his council; period of temporary vows (temporary vows can also be annual); formation; perpetual private vows: admission by the general superior with the consent of his/her council; incardination of clerics in the diocese where they have their residence; dimissorial letters to receive Holy Orders from the bishop of the diocese where the clerics are formed.

C. *Those Responsible for the Formation*

D. *Ongoing Formation*

Chapter VII: The Government of the Association

Authority in the Association (canons 617–619); general principles concerning authority in the Association.

I. The Juridical Structure of the Association

The General Assembly of the Association

Role and authority of the Assembly; exofficio members and elected members: election of the general president; other business which may be dealt with by the General Assembly, etc. When the Association is small, a transitional norm may be introduced giving members in perpetual vows the right to vote in the General Assembly.

The General President

Qualifications required to be elected general president; specify what majority of votes is required for the election (see, for example, canon 119, 1°). The election of the president is chaired by the bishop of the diocese where the General Assembly takes place. Role of the president; his or her personal authority and that exercised with his or her council; president's term of office.

II. Separate Juridical Structure for Each Branch

The General Assembly of Each Branch

Main abilities; constituted of ex officio members and delegated elected members, saying: "The number of delegated members. They must be in perpetual vows. The number of delegated members must not be less than that of ex officio members." Elections by universal vote are not permitted.

Elections: General superior and at least four councilors; qualities required for election as general superior; if the male branch also includes clerics, the general superior must be a cleric; councilors must be in perpetual vows.

When the Association is small, a transitional norm can be introduced that members in perpetual vows have the right to vote in the General Assembly of each branch.

The treasurer and general secretary may be elected in the respective General Assembly or appointed by the general superior with the consent of his council. Specify what majority is required for these elections (see, for example, canon 119, 1°).

Other business which may be dealt with in the General Assembly.

The General Government

General superior; his or her role; his or her authority over each branch.

The general council; matters which require the consent of the council (see also canon 127).

The general treasurer: role. The general secretary: role.

The Local Government

Local superior: election or appointment; required conditions; authority; local council in communities with at least eight members in perpetual vows; in smaller communities all members of perpetual vows form the council.

Canonical erection and suppression of houses (canons 610; 616 §1).

Chapter VIII: Administration of Temporal Goods

Chapter IX: Separation from the Association

The chapter should only consist of the following article: "When the general superior, with the consent of his or her council and with the confirmation of the president, grants a member permission to leave the Association, all ties, rights and obligations deriving from the incorporation cease. In cases of dismissal from the Association, one can follow by analogy the procedure indicated in canons 694–704, with adaptations for the particular case."

Chapter X: Obligation to Observe the Statutes

Statutes for Married Couples

The Statutes can be drawn up taking into account what is written above, with the necessary adaptations according to the specific situation of married laypeople, especially with regard to the topic of vows. In any case, married persons should not be allowed to make vows, but simply a promise to observe their baptismal and matrimonial commitments and their own Statutes, according to the formula established in the Statutes.

2.3 CHALLENGES AND BENEFITS

Such a structure respects the charism of communion of states of life.[185] In fact, consecrated life is recognized in a new way, clerics are fully incorporated — they can likewise be incardinated into the community, if the Holy See grants this faculty — and the laity integrate into it through bonds respecting their identity. Certainly, such varied groups incorporating together pose a challenge, surmountable by the determined commitment of each member to serve fraternal communion and desire a holy life. Moreover, when laypeople, clerics, and consecrated persons become approved as a single canonical identity, the temporal assets belong to the single family, contrary to movements or new communities that, due to the diversity of internal associations and institutes, risk having a

---

[185] See Bertolone, "Nuove comunità e vita consacrata," 40.

divided patrimony, which may lessen the authority of the president of the Ecclesial Family.

Since each branch has its own fraternal life but also seeks communion with the other branches, several elements can ensure strong fraternal bonds between the members of the same branch and with the entire structure: the spiritual patrimony of the foundation, which characterizes its own apostolic way of acting; a specific spirituality nourished by different means (including the Eucharist, Liturgy, retreats); times of formation that bring together all the members of a branch or the entire association; moments of dialogue; meetings of a more informative or decision-making nature; fraternal attention to the human and spiritual growth of each member; and accompanying members as they age.

Conclusion

————— ·——~·⌒——·—————

IN DEALING WITH PASTORAL and canonical issues relating to the new associations, this book is designed to reflect deeper on these realities. Having clarified some institutional questions, necessary to establish their ecclesial position, the movements and new communities will be able to more consciously serve the only mission that Christ has entrusted to the Church.

It is useful to conclude with Pope Francis's encouraging words to the participants of the Third World Congress of Ecclesial Movements and New Communities on November 22, 2014:

> First, it is necessary to preserve the *freshness of your charism*, never lose that freshness, the freshness of your charism, always renewing the "first love" (cf. Rev 2:4).... The newness of your experiences does not consist in methods or forms, or the newness itself, all of which are important, but rather in your willingness to respond with renewed enthusiasm to the Lord's call. Such evangelical courage has allowed for the growth of your Movements and New Communities.... We need always to return to the sources of our charism, and

thus to rediscover the driving force needed to respond to challenges.[186]

At the same time, the Holy Father recommends that the charism of communion, to which many associations refer directly or indirectly, build up the entire ecclesial reality. In fact,

one other consideration we must never forget is that the most precious good, the seal of the Holy Spirit, is communion. This is the supreme blessing that Jesus won for us on the Cross, the grace which the Risen Christ continually implores for us as he reveals to the Father his glorious wounds, "As you, Father, are in me, and I in you, may they also be in us, so that the world may believe that you have sent me" (Jn 17:21). For the world to believe that Jesus is Lord, it needs to see communion among Christians. If, on the other hand, the world sees divisions, rivalries, backbiting, the terrorism of gossip, please . . . if these things are seen, regardless of the cause, how can we evangelize? . . . Real communion cannot exist in Movements or in New Communities unless these are integrated within the greater communion of our Holy Mother, the hierarchical Church. "The whole is greater than the part" (cf. *Evangelii gaudium* 234– 237) and the part only has meaning in relation to the whole. Communion also consists in confronting together and in a united fashion the most pressing questions of our day, such as life, the family, peace, the fight against poverty in all its forms, religious freedom and education.[187]

Confirmed by Peter, let us persevere in hope: "The Movements and New Communities that you represent are moving towards a

---

[186] Francis, Address (November 22, 2014), no. 1.
[187] Ibid., no. 3.

deeper sense of belonging to the Church, a maturity that requires vigilance in the path of daily conversion. This will enable an ever more dynamic and fruitful evangelization.... You have already borne much fruit for the Church and the world. You will bear even greater fruit with the help of the Holy Spirit, who raises up and renews his gifts and charisms, and through the intercession of Mary, who never ceases to assist and accompany her children. Go forward."[188]

[188] Ibid., introduction; no. 3.

APPENDIX

———————————⟿•⟿———————————

SELECTED MESSAGES AND ADDRESSES **of St. John Paul II, Benedict XVI, and Francis to the Ecclesial Movements and New Communities**

John Paul II, Message for the World Congress of the Ecclesial Movements and New Communities, May 27, 1998.

Dear Brothers and Sisters in Christ,

1. "We give thanks to God always for you all, constantly mentioning you in our prayers, remembering before our God and Father your work of faith and labor of love and steadfastness of hope in our Lord Jesus Christ" (1 Thes 1:2–3). These words of the Apostle Paul re-echo in my heart with grateful joy as I send you a warm greeting and assure you of my spiritual closeness in anticipation of our meeting in the Vatican.

I extend an affectionate greeting to the President of the Pontifical Council for the Laity, Cardinal James Francis Stafford; to the Secretary, Bishop Stanislaw Rylko, and to the dicastery's staff. My greeting also goes to the leaders and delegates of the various movements, to the Pastors who are accompanying them and to the distinguished speakers.

During your World Congress, you are addressing the theme: "*Ecclesial Movements: Communion and Mission on the Threshold of the Third Millennium.*" I thank the Pontifical Council for the Laity, which has taken responsibility for promoting and organizing this important meeting, as well as the movements that have promptly and willingly accepted the invitation I extended to them on the Vigil of Pentecost two years ago. On that occasion, I hoped that on the way to the Great Jubilee of the Year 2000, during the year dedicated to the Holy Spirit, they would offer a "joint witness" and "in communion with the Pastors and linked with diocesan programmes, [they would bring] their spiritual, educational and missionary riches to the heart of the Church as a precious experience and proposal of Christian life" (*Homily on the Vigil of Pentecost*, 25 May 1996, n. 7; *L'Osservatore Romano* English edition, 29 May 1996, p. 2).

I deeply hope that your congress and the meeting on 30 May 1998 in St Peter's Square will highlight the fruitful vitality of the movements among the People of God, who are preparing to cross the threshold of the third millennium of the Christian era.

2. I am thinking at this moment of the international conferences organized in Rome in 1981, in Rocca di Papa in 1987 and in Bratislava in 1991. I followed their work attentively, accompanying them with prayer and constant encouragement. From the beginning of my Pontificate, I have given special importance to the progress of ecclesial movements, and I have had the opportunity to appreciate the results of their widespread and growing presence during my pastoral visits to parishes and my apostolic journeys. I have noticed with pleasure their willingness to devote their energies to the service of the See of Peter and the local Churches. I have been able to point to them as something new

that is still waiting to be properly accepted and appreciated. Today I notice, with great joy, that they have a more mature self-knowledge. They represent one of the most significant fruits of that springtime in the Church which was foretold by the Second Vatican Council, but unfortunately has often been hampered by the spread of secularization. Their presence is encouraging because it shows that this springtime is advancing and revealing the freshness of the Christian experience based on personal encounter with Christ. Even in the diversity of their forms, these movements are marked by a common awareness of the "newness" which baptismal grace brings to life, through a remarkable longing to reflect on the mystery of communion with Christ and with their brethren, through sound fidelity to the patrimony of the faith passed on by the living stream of Tradition. This gives rise to a renewed missionary zeal which reaches out to the men and women of our era in the concrete situations where they find themselves, and turns its loving attention to the dignity, needs and destiny of each individual.

These are the reasons for the "*joint witness*" which, thanks to the service you have received from the Pontifical Council for the Laity and in a spirit of friendship, dialogue and collaboration with all the movements, is now given concrete expression at this World Congress and, particularly, in a few days at the eagerly awaited "Meeting" in St Peter's Square. A "joint witness," moreover, which has already emerged and been tested in the arduous preparatory phase of these two events.

The significant presence among you of the superiors and representatives of other dicasteries of the Roman Curia, of Bishops from various continents and nations, of delegates from the International Unions of Superiors General, of the guests of various institutions and associations shows that the whole Church is involved in this endeavor, confirming that the dimension of communion is essential in the life of movements. The ecumenical dimension is also present, made tangible by the participation of fraternal delegates from other Churches and Christian Communions, to whom I address a special greeting.

3. The object of this World Congress is, on the one hand, to *examine the theological nature* and missionary task of the movements and, on the other, to *encourage mutual edification* through the exchange of testimonies and experiences. Your programme thus involves crucial aspects of the life of the movements which the Spirit of Christ has stirred up to give new apostolic fervor to the ecclesial structure. At the opening of your congress, I would like to propose for your consideration several reflections which we will certainly have occasion to emphasize later during the celebration in St Peter's Square on 30 May.

You represent more than 50 movements and new forms of community life, which are the expression of a multifaceted variety of charisms, educational methods and apostolic forms and goals. This multiplicity is lived in the unity of faith, hope and charity, in obedience to Christ and to the Pastors of the Church. Your very existence is a hymn to the unity in diversity desired by the Spirit and gives witness to it. Indeed, in the mystery of communion of the Body of Christ, unity is never a dull homogeneity or a denial of diversity, just as plurality must never become particularism or dispersion. That is why each of your groups deserves to be appreciated for the particular contribution it makes to the life of the Church.

4. What is meant today by "movement"? The term is often used to refer to realities that differ among themselves, sometimes even by reason of their canonical structure. If, on the one hand, that structure certainly cannot exhaust or capture the wealth of forms produced by the life-giving creativity of Christ's Spirit, on the other, it indicates a concrete ecclesial reality with predominantly lay membership, a faith journey and Christian witness which bases its own

pedagogical method on a precise charism given to the person of the founder in specific circumstances and ways.

The charism's own originality, which gives life to a movement, neither claims nor could claim to add anything to the richness of the *depositum fidei*, safeguarded by the Church with passionate fidelity. Nonetheless, it represents a powerful support, a moving and convincing reminder to live the Christian experience fully, with intelligence and creativity. Therein lies the basis for finding adequate responses to the challenges and needs of ever changing times and historical circumstances.

In this light, the charisms recognized by the Church are ways to deepen one's knowledge of Christ and to give oneself more generously to him, while rooting oneself more and more deeply in communion with the entire Christian people. For this reason they deserve attention from every member of the ecclesial community, beginning with the Pastors to whom the care of the particular Churches is entrusted in communion with the Vicar of Christ. Movements can thus make a valuable contribution to the vital dynamics of the one Church founded on Peter in the various local situations, especially in those regions where the *implantatio Ecclesiae* is still in its early stages or subject to many difficulties.

5. I have often had occasion to stress that there is no conflict or opposition in the Church between the *institutional dimension* and the *charismatic dimension*, of which movements are a significant expression. Both are co-essential to the divine constitution of the Church founded by Jesus, because they both help to make the mystery of Christ and his saving work present in the world. Together they aim at renewing in their own ways the self-awareness of the Church, which in a certain sense can be called a "movement" herself, since she is the realization in time and space of the Father's sending of his Son in the power of the Holy Spirit.

I am convinced that my reflections will be given due consideration during the congress, which I accompany with the prayer that it may bear abundant fruit for the benefit of the Church and of all humanity.

With these sentiments, as I look forward to meeting you in St Peter's Square on the Vigil of Pentecost, I cordially impart a special Apostolic Blessing to you and to those you represent.

John Paul II, Address at the Meeting with Ecclesial Movements and New Communities, May 30, 1998.

"Suddenly a sound came from heaven like the rush of a mighty wind, and it filled all the house where they were sitting. And there appeared to them tongues as of fire, distributed and resting on each one of them. And they were all filled with the Holy Spirit" (Acts 2:2–3)

Dear Brothers and Sisters,

1. With these words the Acts of the Apostles bring us into the heart of the Pentecost event; they show us the disciples, who, gathered with Mary in the Upper Room, receive the gift of the Spirit. Thus Jesus' promise is fulfilled and the time of the Church begins. From that time the wind of the Spirit would carry Christ's disciples to the very ends of the earth. It would take them even to martyrdom for their fearless witness to the Gospel.

It is as though what happened in Jerusalem 2,000 years ago were being repeated this evening in this square, the heart of the Christian world. Like the Apostles then, we too find ourselves gathered in a great upper room of Pentecost, longing for the outpouring of the Spirit. Here we would like to profess with the whole Church "the same Spirit ... the same Lord ... the same God who inspires them all in everyone" (1 Cor 12:4–6). This is the atmosphere we wish to relive, imploring the gifts of the Holy Spirit for each of us and for all the baptized people.

2. I greet and thank Cardinal James Francis Stafford, President of the Pontifical Council for the Laity, for the words he has wished to address to me, also in your name, at the beginning of this meeting. With him I greet the Cardinals and Bishops present. I extend an especially grateful greeting to Chiara Lubich, Kiko Argüello, Jean Vanier and Mons. Luigi Giussani for their moving testimonies. With them, I greet the founders and leaders of the new communities and movements represented here. Lastly, I wish to address each of you, brothers and sisters who belong to the individual ecclesial movements. You promptly and enthusiastically accepted the invitation I addressed to you on Pentecost 1996, and have carefully prepared yourselves, under the guidance of the Pontifical Council for the Laity, for this extraordinary meeting which launches us towards the Great Jubilee of the Year 2000.

Today's event is truly unprecedented: for the first time the movements and new ecclesial communities have all gathered together with the Pope. It is the great "*common witness*" I wished for the year which, in the Church's journey to the Great Jubilee, is dedicated to the Holy Spirit. The Holy Spirit is here with us! It is he who is the soul of this marvelous event of ecclesial communion. Truly, "this is the day which the Lord has made; let us rejoice and be glad in it" (Ps 117:24).

3. In Jerusalem, almost 2,000 years ago, on the day of Pentecost, before an astonished and mocking crowd, due to the unexplainable change observed in the Apostles, Peter courageously proclaims: "Jesus of Nazareth, a man attested to you by God ... you crucified and killed by the hands of lawless men. But God raised him up" (Acts 2:22–24). Peter's words express the Church's self-awareness, based on the certainty that Jesus Christ is alive, is working in the present and changes life.

The Holy Spirit, already at work in the creation of the world and in the Old Covenant, reveals himself in the Incarnation and the Paschal Mystery of the Son of God, and in a way "bursts out" at Pentecost to extend the mission of Christ the Lord in time and space. The Spirit thus makes the Church a stream of new life that flows through the history of mankind.

4. With the Second Vatican Council, the Comforter recently gave the Church, which according to the Fathers is the place "where the Spirit flourishes" (*Catechism of the Catholic Church*, n. 749), a renewed Pentecost, instilling a new and unforeseen dynamism.

Whenever the Spirit intervenes, he leaves people astonished. He brings about events of amazing newness; he radically changes persons and history. This was the unforgettable experience of the Second Vatican Ecumenical Council during which, under the guidance of the same Spirit, the Church rediscovered the charismatic dimension as one of her constitutive elements: "It is not only through the sacraments and the ministrations of the Church that the Holy Spirit makes holy the people, leads them and enriches them with his virtues. Allotting his gifts according as he wills (cf. 1 Cor 12:11), he also distributes special graces among the faithful of every rank.... He makes them fit and ready to undertake various tasks and offices for the renewal and building up of the Church" (*Lumen gentium*, n. 12).

The institutional and charismatic aspects are co-essential as it were to the Church's constitution. They contribute, although differently, to the life, renewal and sanctification of God's People. It is from this providential rediscovery of the Church's charismatic dimension that, before and after the Council, a remarkable pattern of growth has been established for ecclesial movements and new communities.

5. Today the Church rejoices at the renewed confirmation of the prophet Joel's words which we have just heard: "I will pour out my Spirit upon all flesh" (Acts 2:17). You, present here, are the tangible proof of this "outpouring" of the Spirit. Each movement is different from the others, but they are all united in the same

communion and for the same mission. Some charisms given by the Spirit burst in like an impetuous wind, which seizes people and carries them to new ways of missionary commitment to the radical service of the Gospel, by ceaselessly proclaiming the truths of faith, accepting the living stream of tradition as a gift and instilling in each person an ardent desire for holiness.

Today, I would like to cry out to all of you gathered here in St Peter's Square and to all Christians: Open yourselves docilely to the gifts of the Spirit! Accept gratefully and obediently the charisms which the Spirit never ceases to bestow on us! Do not forget that every charism is given for the common good, that is, for the benefit of the whole Church.

6. By their nature, charisms are communicative and give rise to that "spiritual affinity between persons" (*Christifideles laici*, n. 24) and that friendship in Christ which is the origin of "movements." The passage from the original charism to the movement happens through the mysterious attraction that the founder holds for all those who become involved in his spiritual experience. In this way movements officially recognized by ecclesiastical authority offer themselves as forms of self-fulfillment and as reflections of the one Church.

Their birth and spread has brought to the Church's life an unexpected newness which is sometimes even disruptive. This has given rise to questions, uneasiness and tensions; at times it has led to presumptions and excesses on the one hand, and on the other, to numerous prejudices and reservations. It was a testing period for their fidelity, an important occasion for verifying the authenticity of their charisms.

Today a new stage is unfolding before you: that of ecclesial maturity. This does not mean that all problems have been solved. Rather, it is a challenge. A road to take. The Church expects from you the "mature" fruits of communion and commitment.

7. In our world, often dominated by a secularized culture which encourages and promotes models of life without God, the faith of many is sorely tested, and is frequently stifled and dies. Thus we see an urgent need for powerful proclamation and solid, in-depth Christian formation. There is so much need today for mature Christian personalities, conscious of their baptismal identity, of their vocation and mission in the Church and in the world! There is great need for living Christian communities! And here are the movements and the new ecclesial communities: they are the response, given by the Holy Spirit, to this critical challenge at the end of the millennium. You are this providential response.

True charisms cannot but aim at the encounter with Christ in the sacraments. The ecclesial realities to which you belong have helped you to rediscover your baptismal vocation, to appreciate the gifts of the Spirit received at Confirmation, to entrust yourselves to God's forgiveness in the sacrament of Reconciliation and to recognize the Eucharist as the source and summit of all Christian life. Thanks to this powerful ecclesial experience, wonderful Christian families have come into being which are open to life, true "domestic churches," and many vocations to the ministerial priesthood and the religious life have blossomed, as well as new forms of lay life inspired by the evangelical counsels. You have learned in the movements and new communities that faith is not abstract talk, nor vague religious sentiment, but new life in Christ instilled by the Holy Spirit.

8. How is it possible to safeguard and guarantee a charism's authenticity? It is essential in this regard that every movement submit to the discernment of the competent ecclesiastical authority. For this reason no charism can dispense with reference and submission to the Pastors of the Church. The Council wrote in clear words: "Those who have charge over the Church should judge the genuiness and proper use of these gifts, through their

office not indeed to extinguish the Spirit, but to test all things and hold fast to what is good (cf. 1 Thes 5:12; 19–21)" (*Lumen gentium*, n. 12). This is the necessary guarantee that you are taking the right road!

In the confusion that reigns in the world today, it is so easy to err, to give in to illusions. May this element of trusting obedience to the Bishops, the successors of the Apostles, in communion with the Successor of Peter never be lacking in the Christian formation provided by your movements! You know the criteria for the ecclesiality of lay associations found in the Apostolic Exhortation *Christifideles laici* (cf. n. 30). I ask you always to adhere to them with generosity and humility, bringing your experiences to the local Churches and parishes, while always remaining in communion with the Pastors and attentive to their direction.

9. Jesus said: "I came to cast fire upon the earth; and would that it were already kindled!" (Lk 12:49). As the Church prepares to cross the threshold of the third millennium, let us accept the Lord's invitation, so that his fire may spread in our hearts and in those of our brothers and sisters.

Today, from this upper room in St Peter's Square, a great prayer rises: Come, Holy Spirit, come and renew the face of the earth! Come with your seven gifts! Come, Spirit of Life, Spirit of Communion and Love! The Church and the world need you. Come, Holy Spirit, and make ever more fruitful the charisms you have bestowed on us. Give new strength and missionary zeal to these sons and daughters of yours who have gathered here. Open their hearts; renew their Christian commitment in the world. Make them courageous messengers of the Gospel, witnesses to the risen Jesus Christ, the Redeemer and Savior of man. Strengthen their love and their fidelity to the Church.

Let us turn our gaze to Mary, Christ's first disciple, Spouse of the Holy Spirit and Mother of the Church, who was with the

Apostles at the first Pentecost, so that she will help us to learn from her fiat docility to the voice of the Spirit.

Today, from this square, Christ says to each of you: "Go into all the world and preach the gospel to the whole creation" (Mk 16:15). He is counting on every one of you, and so is the Church. "Lo," the Lord promises, "I am with you always to the close of the age" (Mt 28:20).

I am with you.

Amen!

Benedict XVI, Message to the Participants of the Second World Congress on Ecclesial Movements and New Communities, May 22, 2006.

Dear Brothers and Sisters,

While we look forward to the Meeting with the members of more than 100 Ecclesial Movements and New Communities, scheduled for Saturday, 3 June, in St Peter's Square, I am pleased to offer you, the representatives of all these ecclesial associations gathered at Rocca di Papa for your World Congress, a warm greeting with the Apostle's words: "May the God of hope fill you with all joy and peace in believing, so that by the power of the Holy Spirit you may abound in hope" (Rom 15:13).

The memory of the previous World Congress of Ecclesial Movements, held in Rome from 26 to 29 May 1998, is still vivid in my mind and in my heart. In my capacity as the then-Prefect of the Congregation for the Doctrine of the Faith I was asked to speak at it, with a lecture on the Theological locus of Ecclesial Movements.

That Congress culminated in the memorable Meeting with beloved Pope John Paul II on 30 May 1998 in St Peter's Square, during which my Predecessor expressed his approval of the Ecclesial

Movements and New Communities, which he described as "signs of hope" for the good of the Church and humanity.

Today, aware of the ground covered since then on the path marked out by the pastoral concern, affection and teachings of John Paul II, I would like to congratulate the Pontifical Council for the Laity in the persons of Archbishop Stanislaw Rylko, President, Bishop Josef Clemens, Secretary, and their coworkers, for the important and worthwhile initiative of this World Congress.

Its theme: "The beauty of being Christian and the joy of communicating it," is inspired by something I said in the Homily inaugurating my Petrine Ministry. This theme is an invitation to reflect on what the essential features of the Christian event are: in fact, we encounter in it the One who in flesh and blood visibly and historically brought to earth the splendor of God's glory.

The words of Psalm 45[44]:2 apply to him: "You are the fairest of the sons of men." And paradoxically, the Prophet's words also refer to him: "He had no form or comeliness that we should look at him, and no beauty that we should desire him" (Is 53:2).

In Christ the beauty of truth and the beauty of love converge; but love, as people know, also calls for the willingness to suffer, a willingness which for those who love one another can even extend to the sacrifice of life (cf. Jn 15:13)! Christ, who is "the beauty of every beauty," as St Bonaventure used to say (*Sermones Dominicales*, 1:7), is made present in the hearts of men and women and attracts them to their vocation which is love. It is thanks to this extraordinary magnetic force that reason is drawn from its torpor and opened to the Mystery. Thus, the supreme beauty of God's merciful love is revealed and at the same time, the beauty of the human being who, created in the image of God, is regenerated by grace and destined to eternal glory.

Down the ages Christianity has been communicated and disseminated thanks to the newness of life of persons and communities capable of bearing an incisive witness of love, unity and joy.

This force itself has set a vast number of people in "motion," from generation to generation. Was it not perhaps the beauty born from faith on the saints' faces that spurred so many men and women to follow in their footsteps?

Basically, this also applies to you: through the founders and initiators of your Movements and Communities you have glimpsed the Face of Christ shining with special brightness and set out on your way.

Christ still continues today to make resound in the hearts of so many that "come, follow me" which can decide their destiny. This normally happens through the witness of those who have had a personal experience of Christ's presence. On the faces and in the words of these "new creatures," his light becomes visible and his invitation audible.

I therefore say to you, dear friends of the Movements: act so as to ensure that they are always schools of communion, groups journeying on in which one learns to live in the truth and love that Christ revealed and communicated to us through the witness of the Apostles, in the heart of the great family of his disciples.

May Jesus' exhortation ceaselessly re-echo in your hearts: "Let your light so shine before men, that they may see your good works and give glory to your Father who is in heaven" (Mt 5:16). Bring Christ's light to all the social and cultural milieus in which you live. Missionary zeal is proof of a radical experience of ever re-newed fidelity to one's charism that surpasses any kind of weary or selfish withdrawal.

Dispel the darkness of a world overwhelmed by the contradic-tory messages of ideologies! There is no valid beauty if there is not a truth to recognize and follow, if love gives way to transitory sentiment, if happiness becomes an elusive mirage or if freedom degenerates into instinct.

How much evil the mania for power, possession and pleasure can spawn in the lives of people and nations! Take the witness of the freedom with which Christ set us free (cf. Gal 5:1) to this troubled world.

The extraordinary fusion between love of God and love of neighbor makes life beautiful and causes the desert in which we often find ourselves living to blossom anew. Where love is expressed as a passion for the life and destiny of others, where love shines forth in affection and in work and becomes a force for the construction of a more just social order, there the civilization is built that can withstand the advance of barbarity.

Become builders of a better world according to the *ordo amoris* in which the beauty of human life is expressed.

Today, the Ecclesial Movements and New Communities are a luminous sign of the beauty of Christ and of the Church, his Bride. You belong to the living structure of the Church. She thanks you for your missionary commitment, for the formative action on behalf of Christian families that you are increasingly developing and for the promotion of vocations to the ministerial priesthood and consecrated life which you nurture among your members.

She is also grateful to you for your readiness not only to accept the active directives of the Successor of Peter, but also of the Bishops of the various local Churches who, with the Pope, are custodians of truth and charity in unity. I trust in your prompt obedience.

Over and above the affirmation of the right to life itself, the edification of the Body of Christ among others must always prevail with indisputable priority.

Movements must approach each problem with sentiments of deep communion, in a spirit of loyalty to their legitimate Pastors.

May you be sustained by participating in the prayer of the Church, whose liturgy is the most exalted expression of the beauty of God's glory, and in a certain way a glimpse of Heaven upon the earth.

I entrust you to the intercession of the One whom we invoke as the *Tota pulchra*, the "All Fair," an ideal of beauty that artists have always sought to reproduce in their works, the "Woman clothed with the sun" (Rv 12:1) in whom human beauty encounters the beauty of God.

With these sentiments, I extend a special Apostolic Blessing to you all as a pledge of my constant affection.

Benedict XVI, Address to the Participants of the Second World Congress on Ecclesial Movements and New Communities, June 3, 2006.

Dear Brothers and Sisters,

You have come to St Peter's Square this evening in really large numbers to take part in the Pentecost Vigil. I warmly thank you. You belong to different peoples and cultures and represent here all the members of the Ecclesial Movements and New Communities, spiritually gathered round the Successor of Peter to proclaim the joy of believing in Jesus Christ and to renew the commitment to be faithful disciples in our time.

I thank you for your participation and address my cordial greeting to each one of you. My affectionate thoughts go in the first place to the Cardinals, to my venerable Brothers in the Episcopate and in the Priesthood and to the men and women Religious.

I greet those in charge of your numerous Ecclesial Associations who show how alive the Holy Spirit's action is among the People of God. I greet the organizers of this extraordinary event, and especially those who work at the Pontifical Council for the Laity with Bishop Josef Clemens, the Secretary, and Archbishop Stanislaw Rylko, the President, to whom I am also grateful for his cordial words at the beginning of the Vespers Liturgy.

A similar meeting that took place in this same Square on 30 May 1998 with beloved Pope John Paul II springs to mind. A great evangelizer of our time, he accompanied and guided you throughout his Pontificate.

He described your Associations and Communities on many occasions as "providential," especially because the Sanctifying Spirit makes use of them to reawaken faith in so many Christian hearts and to reveal to them the vocation they have received with Baptism. He also helps them to be witnesses of hope filled with that fire of love which is bestowed upon us precisely by the Holy Spirit.

Let us ask ourselves now, at this Pentecost Vigil, who or what is the Holy Spirit? How can we recognize him? How do we go to him and how does he come to us? What does he do?

The Church's great Pentecostal hymn with which we began Vespers: "*Veni, Creator Spiritus*... Come, Holy Spirit" gives us a first answer. Here the hymn refers to the first verses of the Bible that describe the creation of the universe with recourse to images.

The Bible says first of all that the Spirit of God was moving over the chaos, over the waters of the abyss.

The world in which we live is the work of the Creator Spirit. Pentecost is not only the origin of the Church and thus in a special way her feast; Pentecost is also a feast of creation. The world does not exist by itself; it is brought into being by the creative Spirit of God, by the creative Word of God.

For this reason Pentecost also mirrors God's wisdom. In its breadth and in the omni-comprehensive logic of its laws, God's wisdom permits us to glimpse something of his Creator Spirit. It elicits reverential awe.

Those very people who, as Christians, believe in the Creator Spirit become aware of the fact that we cannot use and abuse the world and matter merely as material for our actions and desires; that we must consider creation a gift that has not been given to us to be destroyed, but to become God's garden, hence, a garden for men and women.

In the face of the many forms of abuse of the earth that we see today, let us listen, as it were, to the groaning of creation of which St Paul speaks (Rom 8:22); let us begin by understanding the Apostle's words, that creation waits with impatience for the revelation that we are children of God, to be set free from bondage and obtain his splendor.

Dear friends, we want to be these children of God for whom creation is waiting, and we can become them because the Lord has made us such in Baptism. Yes, creation and history—they are waiting for us, for men and women who are truly children of God and behave as such.

If we look at history, we see that creation prospered around monasteries, just as with the reawakening of God's Spirit in human hearts the brightness of the Creator Spirit has also been restored to the earth—a splendor that has been clouded and at times even extinguished by the barbarity of the human mania for power.

Moreover, the same thing happened once again around Francis of Assisi—it has happened everywhere as God's Spirit penetrates souls, this Spirit whom our hymn describes as light, love and strength.

Thus, we have discovered an initial answer to the question as to what the Holy Spirit is, what he does and how we can recognize him. He comes to meet us through creation and its beauty.

However, in the course of human history, a thick layer of dirt has covered God's good creation, which makes it difficult if not impossible to perceive in it the Creator's reflection, although the knowledge of the Creator's existence is reawakened within us ever anew, as it were, spontaneously, at the sight of a sunset over the sea, on an excursion to the mountains or before a flower that has just bloomed.

But the Creator Spirit comes to our aid. He has entered history and speaks to us in a new way. In Jesus Christ, God himself was made man and allowed us, so to speak, to cast a glance at the intimacy of God himself.

And there we see something totally unexpected: in God, an "I" and a "You" exist. The mysterious God is not infinite loneliness, he is an event of love. If by gazing at creation we think we can glimpse the Creator Spirit, God himself, rather like creative mathematics, like a force that shapes the laws of the world and their order, but then, even, also like beauty—now we come to realize: the Creator Spirit has a heart. He is Love.

The Son who speaks to the Father exists and they are both one in the Spirit, who constitutes, so to speak, the atmosphere of giving and loving which makes them one God. This unity of love which is God, is a unity far more sublime than the unity of a last indivisible particle could be. The Triune God himself is the one and only God.

Through Jesus let us as it were cast a glance at God in his intimacy. John, in his Gospel, expressed it like this: "No one has ever seen God; the only Son, who is in the bosom of the Father, he has made him known" (Jn 1:18).

Yet Jesus did not only let us see into God's intimacy; with him, God also emerged, as it were, from his intimacy and came to meet us. This happened especially in his life, passion, death and Resurrection; in his words.

Jesus, however is not content with coming to meet us. He wants more. He wants unification. This is the meaning of the images of the banquet and the wedding.

Not only must we know something about him, but through him we must be drawn to God. For this reason he had to die and be raised, since he is now no longer to be found in any specific place, but his Spirit, the Holy Spirit, emanates from him and enters our hearts, thereby uniting us with Jesus himself and with the Father, the Triune God.

Pentecost is this: Jesus, and through him God himself, actually comes to us and draws us to himself. "He sends forth the Holy Spirit"—this is what Scripture says. What effect does this have?

I would like first of all to pick out two aspects: the Holy Spirit, through whom God comes to us, brings us life and freedom. Let us look at both these things a little more closely.

"I came that they might have life, and have it abundantly," Jesus says in the Gospel of John (10:10). Life and freedom: these are the things for which we all yearn. But what is this—where and how do we find "life"?

I think that the vast majority of human beings spontaneously have the same concept of life as the Prodigal Son of the Gospel. He had his share of the patrimony given to him and then felt free; in the end, what he wanted was to live no longer burdened by the duties of home, but just to live. He wanted everything that life can offer. He wanted to enjoy it to the full—living, only living, immersed in life's abundance, missing none of all the valuable things it can offer.

In the end he found himself caring for pigs and even envying those animals—his life had become so empty and so useless. And his freedom was also proving useless.

When all that people want from life is to take possession of it, it becomes ever emptier and poorer; it is easy to end up seeking refuge in drugs, in the great deception. And doubts surface as to whether, in the end, life is truly a good.

No, we do not find life in this way. Jesus' words about life in abundance are found in the Good Shepherd discourse. His words are set in a double context.

Concerning the shepherd, Jesus tells us that he lays down his life. "No one takes [my life] from me, but I lay it down of my own accord" (cf. Jn 10:18). It is only in giving life that it is found; life is not found by seeking to possess it. This is what we must learn from

Christ; and the Holy Spirit teaches us that it is a pure gift, that it is God's gift of himself. The more one gives one's life for others, for goodness itself, the more abundantly the river of life flows.

Secondly, the Lord tells us that life unfolds in walking with the Shepherd who is familiar with the pasture—the places where the sources of life flow.

We find life in communion with the One who is life in person—in communion with the living God, a communion into which we are introduced by the Holy Spirit, who is called in the hymn of Vespers "*fons vivus*," a living source.

The pasture where the sources of life flow is the Word of God as we find it in Scripture, in the faith of the Church. The pasture is God himself who we learn to recognize in the communion of faith through the power of the Holy Spirit.

Dear friends, the Movements were born precisely of the thirst for true life; they are Movements for life in every sense.

Where the true source of life no longer flows, where people only appropriate life instead of giving it, wherever people are ready to dispose of unborn life because it seems to take up room in their own lives, it is there that the life of others is most at risk.

If we want to protect life, then we must above all rediscover the source of life; then life itself must re-emerge in its full beauty and sublimeness; then we must let ourselves be enlivened by the Holy Spirit, the creative source of life.

The theme of freedom has just been mentioned. The Prodigal Son's departure is linked precisely with the themes of life and freedom. He wanted life and therefore desired to be totally liberated. Being free, in this perspective, means being able to do whatever I like, not being bound to accept any criterion other than and over and above myself. It means following my own desires and my own will alone.

Those who live like this very soon clash with others who want to live the same way. The inevitable consequence of this selfish concept of freedom is violence and the mutual destruction of freedom and life.

Sacred Scripture, on the other hand, connects the concept of freedom with that of sonship. St Paul says: "You did not receive the spirit of slavery to fall back into fear, but you have received the spirit of sonship," through which we cry, "Abba! Father!" (Rom 8:15). What does this mean?

St Paul presupposes the social system of the ancient world in which slaves existed. They owned nothing, so they could not be involved in the proper development of things.

Co-respectively, there were sons who were also heirs and were therefore concerned with the preservation and good administration of their property or the preservation of the State. Since they were free, they also had responsibility.

Leaving aside the sociological background of that time, the principle still holds true: freedom and responsibility go hand in hand. True freedom is demonstrated in responsibility, in a way of behaving in which one takes upon oneself a shared responsibility for the world, for oneself and for others.

The son, to whom things belong and who, consequently, does not let them be destroyed, is free. All the worldly responsibilities of which we have spoken are nevertheless partial responsibilities for a specific area, a specific State, etc.

The Holy Spirit, on the other hand, makes us sons and daughters of God. He involves us in the same responsibility that God has for his world, for the whole of humanity. He teaches us to look at the world, others and ourselves with God's eyes. We do not do good as slaves who are not free to act otherwise, but we do it because we are personally responsible for the world; because we love truth and goodness, because we love God himself and therefore, also his creatures. This is the true freedom to which the Holy Spirit wants to lead us.

The Ecclesial Movements want to and must be schools of freedom, of this true freedom. Let us learn in them this true freedom, not the freedom of slaves that aims to cut itself a slice of the cake that belongs to everyone even if this means that some do not get any.

We want the true, great freedom, the freedom of heirs, the freedom of children of God. In this world, so full of fictitious forms of freedom that destroy the environment and the human being, let us learn true freedom by the power of the Holy Spirit; to build the school of freedom; to show others by our lives that we are free and how beautiful it is to be truly free with the true freedom of God's children.

The Holy Spirit, in giving life and freedom, also gives unity. These are three gifts that are inseparable from one another. I have already gone on too long; but let me say a brief word about unity.

To understand it, we might find a sentence useful which at first seems rather to distance us from it. Jesus said to Nicodemus, who came to him with his questions by night: "The wind blows where it wills" (Jn 3:8). But the Spirit's will is not arbitrary. It is the will of truth and goodness.

Therefore, he does not blow from anywhere, now from one place and then from another; his breath is not wasted but brings us together because the truth unites and love unites.

The Holy Spirit is the Spirit of Jesus Christ, the Spirit who unites the Father with the Son in Love, which in the one God he gives and receives. He unites us so closely that St Paul once said: "You are all one in Jesus Christ" (Gal 3:28).

With his breath, the Holy Spirit impels us towards Christ. The Holy Spirit acts corporeally; he does not only act subjectively or "spiritually."

The Risen Christ said to his disciples, who supposed that they were seeing only a "spirit": "It is I myself; touch me, and see; for a spirit has not flesh and bones as you see that I have" (cf. Lk 24:39).

This applies for the Risen Christ in every period of history. The Risen Christ is not a ghost, he is not merely a spirit, a thought, only an idea.

He has remained incarnate—it is the Risen One who took on our flesh—and always continues to build his Body, making us his Body. The Spirit breathes where he wills, and his will is unity embodied, a unity that encounters the world and transforms it.

In his Letter to the Ephesians, St Paul tells us that this Body of Christ, which is the Church, has joints (cf. 4:16) and even names them: they are apostles, prophets, evangelists, pastors and teachers (cf. 4:12). In his gifts, the Spirit is multifaceted—we see it here. If we look at history, if we look at this assembly here in St Peter's Square, then we realize that he inspires ever new gifts; we see how different are the bodies that he creates and how he works bodily ever anew.

But in him multiplicity and unity go hand in hand. He breathes where he wills. He does so unexpectedly, in unexpected places and in ways previously unheard of. And with what diversity and corporality does he do so! And it is precisely here that diversity and unity are inseparable.

He wants your diversity and he wants you for the one body, in union with the permanent orders—the joints—of the Church, with the successors of the Apostles and with the Successor of St Peter.

He does not lessen our efforts to learn the way of relating to one another; but he also shows us that he works with a view to the one body and in the unity of the one body. It is precisely in this way that unity obtains its strength and beauty.

May you take part in the edification of the one body! Pastors must be careful not to extinguish the Spirit (cf. 1 Thes 5:19) and you will not cease to bring your gifts to the entire community.

Once again, the Spirit blows where he wills. But his will is unity. He leads us towards Christ through his Body.

"From Christ," St Paul tells us, "the whole body, joined and knit together by every joint with which it is supplied, when each part is working properly, makes bodily growth and upbuilds itself in love" (Eph 4:16).

The Holy Spirit desires unity, he desires totality. Therefore, his presence is finally shown above all in missionary zeal.

Anyone who has come across something true, beautiful and good in his life — the one true treasure, the precious pearl — hastens to share it everywhere, in the family and at work, in all the contexts of his life.

He does so without any fear, because he knows he has received adoption as a son; without any presumption, for it is all a gift; without discouragement, for God's Spirit precedes his action in people's "hearts" and as a seed in the most diverse cultures and religions.

He does so without restraint, for he bears a piece of good news which is for all people and for all the peoples.

Dear friends, I ask you to collaborate even more, very much more, in the Pope's universal apostolic ministry, opening doors to Christ.

This is the Church's best service for men and women and especially for the poor, so that the person's life, a fairer order in society and peaceful coexistence among the nations may find in Christ the cornerstone on which to build the genuine civilization, the civilization of love.

The Holy Spirit gives believers a superior vision of the world, of life, of history, and makes them custodians of the hope that never disappoints.

Let us pray to God the Father, therefore, through Our Lord Jesus Christ, in the grace of the Holy Spirit, so that the celebration of the Solemnity of Pentecost may be like an ardent flame and a blustering wind for Christian life and for the mission of the whole Church.

I place the intentions of your Movements and Communities in the heart of the Most Blessed Virgin Mary, present in the Upper Room together with the Apostles; may she be the one who implores God to grant them.

Upon all of you I invoke an outpouring of the gifts of the Spirit, so that in our time too, we may have the experience of a renewed Pentecost. Amen!

Francis, Address to the Participants in the Third World Congress of Ecclesial Movements and New Communities, November 22, 2014.

Dear brothers and sisters, Good morning!

I offer cordial greetings to all of you taking part in this Congress sponsored by the Pontifical Council for the Laity. I thank Cardinal Rylko for his words, as well as Archbishop Clemens. At the heart of your deliberations in these days are two elements which are essential for Christian life: *conversion* and *mission*. These are intimately connected. In fact, without an authentic conversion of heart and mind, the Gospel cannot be proclaimed; at the same time, if we are not open to mission, conversion is not possible and faith becomes sterile. The Movements and New Communities that you represent are moving towards a deeper sense of belonging to the Church, a maturity that requires vigilance in the path of daily conversion. This will enable an ever more dynamic and fruitful evangelization. I would like, therefore, to offer you a few suggestions for your journey of faith and ecclesial life.

1. First, it is necessary to preserve the *freshness of your charism*, never lose that freshness, the freshness of your charism, always renewing the "first love" (cf. Rev 2:4). As time goes by, there is a greater temptation to become comfortable, to become hardened in set ways of doing things, which, while reassuring, are nonetheless sterile. There is the temptation to cage in the Holy Spirit: this is a temptation! However, "realities are more important than ideas" (cf. *Evangelii Gaudium* 231–233); even if a certain institutionalization of the charism is necessary for its survival, we ought not delude ourselves into thinking that external structures can guarantee the working of the Holy Spirit. The newness of your experiences does not consist in methods or forms, or the newness itself, all of which are important, but rather in your willingness to respond with renewed enthusiasm to the Lord's call. Such evangelical courage has allowed for the growth of your Movements and New Communities. If forms and methods become ends in themselves, they become ideological, removed from reality which is constantly developing; closed to the newness of the Spirit, such rigid forms and methods will eventually stifle the very charism which gave them life. We need always to return to the sources of our charism, and thus to rediscover the driving force needed to respond to challenges. You have not been schooled in such a spirituality. You have not attended an institution of spirituality in this way. You are not simply a small group. No! You are rather a movement, always on the way, always in movement, always open to God's surprises which are in harmony with the first call of the movement, namely the founding charism.

2. A further issue concerns the *way of welcoming and accompanying* men and women of today, in particular, the youth (cf. *Evangelii Gaudium* 105–106). We are part of a wounded humanity—and we must be honest in saying this—in which all of the educational institutions, especially the most important one, the family, are

experiencing grave difficulties almost everywhere in the world. Men and women today experience serious identity problems and have difficulty making proper choices; as a result, they tend to be conditioned and to delegate important decisions about their own lives to others. We need to resist the temptation of usurping individual freedom, of directing them without allowing for their growth in genuine maturity. Every person has their own time, their own path, and we must accompany this journey. Moral or spiritual progress which manipulates a person's immaturity is only an apparent success, and one destined to fail. It is better to achieve less and move forward without seeking attention. Christian education, rather, requires a patient accompaniment which is capable of waiting for the right moment for each person, as the Lord does with each one of us. The Lord is patient with us! Patience is the only way to love truly and to lead others into a sincere relationship with the Lord.

3. One other consideration we must never forget is that the most precious good, the seal of the Holy Spirit, is *communion*. This is the supreme blessing that Jesus won for us on the Cross, the grace which the Risen Christ continually implores for us as he reveals to the Father his glorious wounds, "As you, Father, are in me, and I in you, may they also be in us, so that the world may believe that you have sent me" (Jn 17:21). For the world to believe that Jesus is Lord, it needs to see communion among Christians. If, on the other hand, the world sees divisions, rivalries, backbiting, the terrorism of gossip, please ... if these things are seen, regardless of the cause, how can we evangelize? Remember this further principle: "Unity prevails over conflict" (*Evangelii Gaudium* 226–230), because our brothers and sisters are always of greater value than our personal attitudes; indeed, it is for our brothers and sisters that Christ has shed his blood (1 Pet 1:18–19); it has not been shed for my ideas! In addition, real communion

cannot exist in Movements or in New Communities unless these are integrated within the greater communion of our Holy Mother, the hierarchical Church. "The whole is greater than the part" (cf. *Evangelii Gaudium* 234–237), and the part only has meaning in relation to the whole. Communion also consists in confronting together and in a united fashion the most pressing questions of our day, such as life, the family, peace, the fight against poverty in all its forms, religious freedom and education. In particular, New Movements and Communities are called to coordinate their efforts in caring for those wounded by a globalized mentality which places consumption at the center, neglecting God and those values which are essential for life.

In order to attain ecclesial maturity, therefore, maintain — I say again — the *freshness of your charism*, respect the *freedom of each person*, and always strive for *communion*. Do not forget, however, that to reach this goal, conversion must be missionary: the strength to overcome temptations and insufficiencies comes from the profound joy of proclaiming the Gospel, which is the foundation of your charisms. In fact, "when the Church summons Christians to take up the task of evangelization, she is simply pointing to the source of authentic personal fulfilment" (*Evangelii Gaudium* 10), the true motivation for renewal of one's own life, since all mission is a sharing in the mission of Christ who always precedes and accompanies us in the work of evangelization.

Dear brothers and sisters, you have already borne much fruit for the Church and the world. You will bear even greater fruit with the help of the Holy Spirit, who raises up and renews his gifts and charisms, and through the intercession of Mary, who never ceases to assist and accompany her children. Go forward, always in movement ... never stop but always keep moving! I assure you of my prayers and I ask you to pray for me — I have great need, truly — and I cordially impart to each of you my blessing.

I now ask you, together, to pray to Our Lady who had the experience of keeping alive the freshness of the first encounter with God, of moving forward in humility, always being on the way, respecting each person's time. She never tired of having this missionary heart.

Francis, Address to the Participants in the Meeting of Moderators of Lay Associations, Ecclesial Movements and New Communities, September 16, 2021.

Dear brothers and sisters, good morning and welcome!

I cordially greet His Eminence Cardinal Kevin Farrell, and I thank him for the words he addressed to me. And thank you to you all, for being present despite the inconveniences caused by the pandemic and sometimes by the bad feeling that this decree has perhaps sown in some people's hearts. I also greet and thank those who are participating via video link, most of whom were unable to travel due to the limitations still in force in many countries. I don't know how the Secretary managed to return from Brazil! Later you will have to explain to me.

1. I wished to be here, first and foremost, to say thank you! Thank you for your presence as laypersons, men and women, young and elderly, committed to living and bearing witness to the Gospel in the everyday realities of life, in your work, in many different contexts—education, social commitment, and so on, in the street, at railway terminals, there, you were all there—this is the vast field of your apostolate, it is your evangelization. And we must understand that evangelization is a mandate that comes from Baptism, the Baptism that makes us priests together, in the priesthood of Christ; the priestly population, no? And we must not wait for the priest to come, for the priest to evangelize, the missionary … Yes, they do great good, but whoever has been baptized has the

task of evangelizing. And you have reawakened this with your movements. And this is very good. Thank you.

During recent months, you have seen with your own eyes and touched with your hands the sufferings and anguish of many men and women, due to the pandemic, especially in the poorest countries, where many of you are present. One of you spoke with me about this. So much poverty and destitution … I think of us here in the Vatican—everything is good, isn't it?—who complain when our meal is not cooked well, when … there are people who have nothing to eat. I am grateful to you because you have not stopped; you have not stopped bringing your solidarity, your help, your evangelical testimony even during the hardest months, when the level of contagion was very high. Despite the restrictions due to the necessary preventative measures, you did not give up: on the contrary, I know that many of you redoubled your efforts, adapting to the real situations you have, and had before you, with that creativity that comes from love, because those who feel loved by the Lord love without measure. We have seen this "without measure" in so many religious sisters, in many consecrated women, in many priests and in many bishops. I am thinking of a bishop who ended up intubated because he always wanted to stay with his people. He is now slowly recovering. You and all the people of God stood together in this, and you were there. None of you said, "No, I can't go, because my founder thinks differently." So, no founder: here there was the Gospel that called, and everyone went forth. Thank you very much. You have been witnesses to "that (blessed) common belonging, of which we cannot be deprived: our belonging as brothers and sisters." There are no half measures.

2. As members of associations of the faithful, of international ecclesial movements and other communities, you have a genuinely ecclesial mission. With devotion you endeavor to live out and make fruitful those charisms that the Holy Spirit, through your

founders, granted to all the members of your groups, to the benefit of the Church and of the many men and women to whom you dedicate yourselves in the apostolate. I think especially of those who, finding themselves in the existential peripheries of our societies, experience abandonment and solitude in their own flesh, and suffer as a result of their many material needs and of moral and spiritual poverty. It will do us all good to remember every day not only the poverty of others, but also, and above all, our own. There is something about Mother Teresa that often comes to mind, no? Yes, she was a religious sister, but this happens to us all if we are on the street. When you go to pray and feel nothing. I call it that spiritual atheism, where everything is dark, everything seems to say: "I have failed, this is not the way, this is just an illusion" ... but, the temptation, of that atheism, when it comes in prayer. Poor Mother Teresa suffered greatly because it is the devil's revenge that we go there, to the peripheries where Jesus is, indeed where Jesus was born, wasn't He? We prefer a sophisticated Gospel, a distilled Gospel. And this is not the Gospel. The Gospel is this. Thank you. It will do good to us all to think of those forms of poverty.

You are too, though with the limits and sins of every day—thanks to God, that we are sinners and that God gives us the grace of recognizing our sins and also the grace of asking or going to the confessor. This is a great grace: do not lose it ... though with these limits, you are a clear sign of the vitality of the Church. You represent a missionary force and a presence of prophecy that gives us hope for the future. You too, along with the pastors and all the other lay faithful, have the responsibility of building the future of the holy faithful people of God. But always remember that building the future does not mean coming out of the today that we are living in! On the contrary, the future must be prepared here and now, it is "in the kitchen," learning to listen and to discern the present time with honesty and courage, and with the willingness to engage in a constant encounter with the Lord, a constant personal conversion. Otherwise, one runs the risk of living in a "parallel world," distilled, distant, far from the real challenges of society, of culture and of all those people who live alongside you and who await your Christian witness. Indeed, belonging to an association, a movement or a community, especially if they refer to a charism, should not lock us up "safe and sound," make us feel secure, as if there were no need for any response to challenges and changes. We Christians are always all on the move, always in conversion, always in discernment. And so often we find so-called "pastoral agents;" be they bishops, priests, nuns, compromised laypeople. I do not like that word. The laity is "compromised" or "not compromised." The laity are active in something. But there are some who confuse the journey with a tourist trip or confuse the journey with always turning in on oneself, without being able to move forward. The Gospel journey is not a tourist trip. It is a challenge: every step is a challenge and every step is a call from God, every step is — as we say in our country — "putting meat on the grill." Always moving forward. We are always on the move, always in conversion, always discerning to do God's will. Thinking we are "new" in the Church — this is a temptation that often happens to new congregations or movements — and therefore not in need of change, can become a false security. Even novelties soon get old! For this reason, the charism to which we belong must be furthered more and more, and we must always reflect together in order to incarnate it in the new situations we live in. To do this, great docility is required of us, and great humility, in order to recognize our limitations and accept to change outdated ways of doing and thinking, or methods of the apostolate that are no longer effective, or forms of organization of internal life that have proved inadequate or even harmful. For example, this is one of the services that General Chapters always provide to us, when they are not good you have to revise them, right?… in the assembly, I don't know what you call them, I am not sure.

But now we come to the point, to what you have been waiting for.

3. The Decree on International Associations of the Faithful, promulgated on 11 June this year, is a step in this direction. But does this decree imprison us? Does it deny us our freedom? No, this Decree urges us to accept some changes and to prepare the future, starting from the present. At the origin of this decree there is not some theory of the Church or lay associations that you want to apply or impose, is there? No, there is not. It is the very reality of the last few decades that has shown us the need for the changes that the Decree asks of us. And I will tell you something about this experience of the last few decades of the post-Council period. In the Congregation for Religious they are studying the religious congregations, the associations that were established in this period. It's curious, it's very curious. Many, many, with a novelty that was great, ended up in very difficult situations: they have ended up under apostolic visitation, they have ended up with terrible sins, they have been placed under commission … And they are performing a study. I do not know if you can publish this, but you know better than I do from clerical chatter what these situations are. But there are many and not only are these great ones that we know, which are scandalous, the things that they did to seem like an entirely different Church—it seemed that way, didn't it? The Redemptorists …—but also small ones. In my country, for example, three of them have already been dissolved and all of them have ended up in the dirtiest things. They offered salvation, didn't they? They seemed to … Always with that thread of disciplinary rigidity. That's important. And this has led me … And this reality of the last decades has shown us a series of changes to help,

changes that the Decree asks of us. Today, therefore, starting from that Decree, you are focusing on a theme that is important not only for each of you, but for the whole Church: "The responsibility of governance in lay groups. An ecclesial service." To govern is to serve. The exercise of governance within associations and movements is a theme that is particularly close to my heart, especially considering – what I said earlier – the cases of abuse of various kinds that have occurred in these realities and that always find their root in the abuse of power. This is the origin: the abuse of power. Not infrequently the Holy See, in recent years, has had to intervene, launching difficult processes of rehabilitation. And I am thinking not only of these very ugly situations, which make a lot of noise, but also of the diseases that come from the weakening of the founding charism, which becomes lukewarm and loses its capacity for attraction.

4. The positions of governance entrusted to you in the lay groups to which you belong are none other than a call to serve. But what does it mean for a Christian to serve? On a number of occasions, I have had the opportunity to point out two obstacles that a Christian may encounter on his journey and which prevent him from becoming a true servant of God and of others (cf. Morning meditation at the Casa Santa Marta, 8 November 2016).

5. The first is the "lust for power," when this lust for power makes you change the nature of service in governance. How many times have we made others feel our "lust for power"? Jesus taught us that the one who commands must become like the one who serves (cf. Lk 22:24–26) and that "Whoever wants to be first must be last of all and servant of all" (Mk 9:35). Jesus, in other words, overturns the values of worldliness, of the world.

Our desire for power is expressed in many ways in the life of the Church; for example, when we believe, by virtue of the role we have, that we have to take decisions on all aspects of the life of our association, diocese, parish, congregation. We delegate tasks and responsibilities for certain areas to others, but only in theory! In practice, however, delegation to others is emptied by the eagerness to be everywhere. And this desire for power nullifies all forms of subsidiarity. This attitude is ugly and ends up emptying the ecclesial body of its strength. It is a bad way of "disciplining." And we have seen it. So many, and I'm thinking of the congregations I know the most, superiors, superiors general who eternalize themselves in power and do a thousand, a thousand things to get re-elected again and again, right? Even changing the constitutions . . . And behind it there is a desire for power. This does not help; this is the beginning of the end of an association, of a congregation.

Perhaps some may think that this "desire" does not concern them, that it does not happen in their own association. Let us bear in mind that the Decree on International Associations of the Faithful is not only addressed to some of the realities present here, but is for all, without exception. For all. There are not some who are more or less good than others, perfect or not: all ecclesial realities are called to conversion, to understand and implement the spirit that animates the provisions given to us in the Decree. I have two images of this. Two historical images. That nun who was at the entrance to the Chapter and said: "If you vote for me, I will do this for you." They buy power. And then, a case that seems strange to me, no?, such as: "The spirit of the founder has descended upon me." But it sounds like a prophecy from Isaiah, doesn't it? "He has given him to me! I must go forth alone or only because the founder has given me his mantle, like Elijah to Elisha. And you, yes, do the voting, but I am in charge." And this happens! I'm not talking about fantasies. This happens today and in the Church.

The experience of being close to your realities has taught us that it is beneficial and necessary to provide for a rotation in posts of governance, and for the representation of all members in your elections. Even in the context of consecrated life there are religious institutes which, by keeping the same people in posts of governance, have not prepared for the future; they have allowed abuses to creep in and are now experiencing great difficulties. I am thinking, you will not know it [ever?] but they have an institute where their leader was called [Amabilia?]. The institute ended up being called 'hatebilia' because the members realized that the woman was a "Hitler" in a dress.

6. Then there is another obstacle to true Christian service, and this one is very subtle: disloyalty. We encounter it when someone wants to serve the Lord but also serves other things that are not the Lord. And behind other things, there is always money, is there not? It is a bit like playing a double game! We say in words that we want to serve God and others, but in fact we serve our ego, and we bend to our desire to appear, to obtain recognition, appreciation … Let us not forget that true service is gratuitous and unconditional, it knows no calculations or demands. Also, true service habitually forgets the things it has done to serve others. And it happens, doesn't it? All of you have had this experience, when you are thanked, and you ask "What for?"— "For what you have done …" — "But what have I done?"… And then it comes to mind. It is service. Full stop.

And we fall into the trap of disloyalty when we present ourselves to others as the sole interpreters of the charisma, the sole heirs of our association or movement—that case I mentioned earlier—or when, believing ourselves to be indispensable, we do all we can to hold posts for life; or again when we claim to decide *a priori* who our successor should be. Does this happen? Yes, it happens. And more often than we think. No one is master of the gifts received for the good of the Church—we are administrators—, no one should suffocate them, let them grow with me or with what comes after me. Instead, each one, where he or she is placed by the Lord, is called to make them grow, to make them and bear fruit, confident in the fact that it is God who works all things in all people (cf. 1 Cor 12:6) and that our true good bears fruit in ecclesial communion.

7. Dear friends, in carrying out the role of governance entrusted to us, let us learn to be true servants of the Lord and of our brothers and sisters, let us learn to say "we are unworthy servants" (Lk 17:10). Let us keep in mind this expression of humility, of docility to God's will, which does so much good to the Church and recalls the right attitude for working in it: humble service, of which Jesus gave us the example, washing the disciples' feet (cf. Jn 13:3–17; *Angelus*, 6 October 2019).

8. In the Dicastery document reference is made to the founders. This seems very wise. But, founders should not be changed; keep going forward. Simplifying a little, I would say that we need to distinguish, in ecclesial movements (and also in religious congregations), between those that are in the process of formation and those that have already acquired a certain organic and juridical stability. They are two different realities. The former also, the institutes, the former have a living founder or foundress.

Although all institutes—whether religious or lay movements—have the duty to verify, in assemblies or chapters, the state of the foundational charism and make the necessary changes in their own legislation (which will then be approved by the respective Dicastery), in institutes in formation—and I say in formation in the broadest sense; institutes that have a living founder, and for this reason the Decree speaks of the founder for life, doesn't it? Therefore, the document speaks of a certain stability of the superiors during this phase. It is important to make this distinction in order to be able to move more freely in discernment.

We are living members of the Church and for this we need to trust in the Holy Spirit, who acts in the life of every association, of every member, acts in each one of us. Hence the trust in the discernment of charisms entrusted to the authority of the Church. Be aware of the apostolic power and prophetic gift that are handed over to you today in a renewed way.

Thank you for listening. And one thing: when I read the draft of the Decree, which I then signed—the first draft—, I thought. "But this is too rigid! It lacks life, it lacks ...." But, dear friends, that's the language of canon law! And here it is a thing of law, it is a thing of language. But we must, as I have tried to do, see what this language, the law, means. That is why I wanted to explain it well. And also to explain the temptations that lie behind it, which we have seen and which do so much harm to the movements and also to religious and lay institutes.

Thank you for listening, and thank you to the Dicastery for the Laity, the Family and Life for organizing this meeting. I wish you all good work and a good meeting. Say whatever comes to you from the heart in this. Ask the things you want to ask, clarify situations. This meeting is for doing this, to build up the Church, for us. And do not forget to pray for me, because I need it. It is not easy to be Pope, but God helps. God always helps.

Bibliography

Anatrella, Tony. *Développer la vie communautaire dans l'Église: L'exemple des Communautés nouvelles.* Dijon: Echelle Jacob, 2014.

Aquinas, St. Thomas. *Summa Theologica.*

Balog, Marta. "Charisme fondateur." *Studia canonica* 50 (2016): 165–174.

Benedict XVI. Address to Bishops and Representatives of Ecclesial Movements and New Communities. May 17, 2008.

———. Address to the Bishop-Friends of the Focolare Movement and the Sant'Egidio Community. February 8, 2007.

———. Address to the German Bishops. August 21, 2005.

———. Apostolic Exhortation *Sacramentum Caritatis* on the Eucharist as the Source and Summit of the Church's Life and Mission. February 22, 2007.

———. Apostolic Exhortation *Verbum Domini* on the Word of God in the Life and Mission of the Church. September 30, 2010.

————. Letter Proclaiming a Year for Priests. June 16, 2009.

————. *Light of the World: The Pope, the Church, and the Signs of the Times; A Conversation with Peter Seewald.* San Francisco: Ignatius Press, 2010.

————. Message to the Participants of the Second World Congress on Ecclesial Movements and New Communities. May 22, 2006.

————. *Regina Caeli.* June 4, 2006.

Bertolone, Vincenzo. "Nuove comunità e vita consacrata." In *Nuove forme di vita consacrata.* Edited by R. Fusco and G. Rocca, 39–53. Rome: Urbaniana University Press, 2010.

Beyer, Jean. "Motus ecclesiales." *Periodica de re morali, canonica, liturgica* 75 (1986): 613–637.

————. "Vita associativa e corresponsabilità ecclesiale." *Vita consacrata* 26 (1990): 923–941.

Camurça, Marcelo, Brenda Carranza, and Cecília Mariz. *Novas comunidades católicas: Em busca do espaço pós-moderno.* Aparecida: Ideias & Letras, 2009.

Canadian Conference of Catholic Bishops. *New Ecclesial Movements and Associations.* September 5, 2006. Accessed on January 22, 2022. https://www.cccb.ca/document/new-ecclesial-movements-associations/.

Carballo, José Rodríguez. "El Vaticano està investigando a una decena de fundadores por abusos o gestión económica." Interview by Darío Menor. *Vida Nueva.* July 30, 2021.

Carriquiry, Guzmán. "The Ecclesial Movements in the Religious and Cultural Context of the Present Day." In *The Ecclesial Movements in the Pastoral Concern of the Bishops.* Edited by

Pontifical Council for the Laity, 47–69. Vatican City: Pontificium Consilium pro Laicis, 2000.

Casey, Maria. "Associations of Christ's Faithful: Possibilities for the Future." *Studia canonica* 41 (2007): 65–90.

Cattaneo, Arturo. "Los movimientos eclesiales: cuestiones eclesiológicas y canónicas." *Ius Canonicum* 76 (1998): 571–594.

————. "The Relationship between the Parish and Ecclesial Movements." Interview on *ZENIT.* December 17, 2004; English version January 10, 2005.

Chagas Júnior, João W.R. *Uma obra nova para um novo tempo: A espiritualidade da Comunidade Católica Shalom.* Fortaleza: Edições Shalom, 2009.

Coda, Piero. "The Ecclesial Movements, Gift of the Spirit: A Theological Reflection." In *Movements in the Church: Proceedings of the World Congress of the Ecclesial Movements, Rome, 27–29 May, 1998.* Edited by Pontifical Council for the Laity, 75–102. Vatican City: Pontificium Consilium pro Laicis, 1999.

Colombo, Marcelo. "Los nuevos movimientos eclesiales y su encuadramiento canónico en la Iglesia particular." *Anuario Argentino de Derecho Canónico* 14 (2007): 89–130.

Comité canonique français des religieux. *Vie religieuse, érémitisme, consécration des vierges, communautés nouvelles.* Paris: Cerf, 1993.

Committee on Divine Worship of the United States Conference of Catholic Bishops (USCCB). *Stewards of the Tradition: Fifty Years After "Sacrosanctum Concilium."* n.p. USCCB, 2013.

Congregation for Bishops. Directives *Mutuae relationes* for the Mutual Relations between Bishops and Religious in the Church. May 14, 1978.

Congregation for the Clergy. Instruction *The Pastoral Conversion of the Parish Community in the Service of the Evangelizing Mission of the Church*. July 20, 2020.

Congregation for Divine Worship. *General Instruction on the Liturgy of the Hours*. February 2, 1971.

Congregation for the Doctrine of the Faith. Letter *Iuvenescit Ecclesia* to the Bishops of the Catholic Church Regarding the Relationship between Hierarchical and Charismatic Gifts in the Life and the Mission of the Church. May 15, 2016.

———. Letter on Some Aspects of Christian Meditation. October 15, 1989.

Congregation for Institutes of Consecrated Life and Societies of Apostolic Life. *Criteria for the Approval of New Forms of Consecrated Life*. January 26, 1990.

———. Directives on Formation in Religious Institutes. February 2, 1990.

———. Letter *Consecration and Secularity* to the Bishops of the Catholic Church Regarding the Secular Institutes. June 4, 2017.

Congregation of Sacred Rites. Instruction *Musicam Sacram* on Music in the Liturgy. March 5, 1967.

Conseil Permanent de l'Épiscopat Français. *Points de repère proposés aux évêques de France pour accompagner une communauté nouvelle. Notamment lors de l'élaboration de ses statuts*. June17, 1987.

Cordes, Paul Josef. *Benedetto XVI ispira i nuovi movimenti e le realtà ecclesiali: Il punto sulla situazione teologico-pastorale.* Vatican City: Libreria Editrice Vaticana, 2012.

Corecco, Eugenio. *Ius et communio.* Casale Monferrato: Piemme, 1997.

de Almeida, Silvio Afonso. *Obra nova: O surgimento de novos carísmas.* São José dos Campos: ComDeus, 2008.

Delgado Galindo, Miguel. "Le don de soi dans les mouvements ecclésiaux." Lecture presented at the Study Day on "Consecration in Ecclesial Movements and in New Communities—Theological and Juridical Aspects." Budapest, April 25, 2009.

———. *Movimenti ecclesiali, ministero petrino e apostolicità della Chiesa.* Rome: VivereIn, 2007.

De Paolis, Velasio. "Le nuove forme di vita consacrata." In *Nuove forme di vita consacrata.* Edited by R. Fusco and G. Rocca, 19–38. Rome: Urbaniana University Press, 2010.

———. *La vita consacrata nella Chiesa.* Venice: Marcianum Press, 2010.

de Sousa, Ronaldo José. *Comunidades de vida: Panorama de um fenômeno religioso moderno.* Aparecida: Editora Santuário, 2013.

Dicastery for Laity, Family, and Life. General Decree *Associations of the Faithful.* June 3, 2021.

Dimas dos Santos, Elias. *Novas comunidades: Dom da Trindade.* São Paulo: Edições Loyola, 2003.

Dortel-Claudot, Michel. *Les communautés nouvelles.* Paris: CEF, 1991.

Donneaud, Henry. "La Communauté des Béatitudes: De l'appel monastique au témoignage missionnaire." *Bulletin de littérature ecclésiastique* 116 (2015): 99–116.

Echeverría, Juan José. "Los movimientos eclesiales en los albores del siglo XXI." *Revista Española de Derecho Canónico* 58 (2001): 577–616.

Ephraim. *Rains of the Late Season: The Holy Spirit at the Birth of a New Community*. Middlegreen: Saint Paul, 1992.

Faggioli, Massimo. *The Rising Laity: Ecclesial Movements since Vatican II*. New York: Paulist Press, 2016.

———. *Sorting Out Catholicism: A Brief History of the New Ecclesial Movements*. Collegeville, MN: Liturgical Press, 2014.

Ferreira, Wagner. *A formação da consciência moral nas novas comunidades*. São Paulo: Editora Canção Nova, 2011.

———. *As novas comunidades no contexto sociocultural contemporâneo*. São Paulo: Editora Canção Nova, 2011.

Forte, Bruno. *Laicato e laicità: Saggi ecclesiologici*. Casale Monferrato: Marietti, 1986.

Francis. Address at Vespers in Asunción, Paraguay. July 11, 2015.

———. Address to the Communion and Liberation Movement. March 7, 2015.

———. Address to the Members of the Cursillos in Christianity in Italy. May 28, 2022.

———. Address to the Participants in the General Chapter of the Missionary Sons of the Immaculate Heart of Mary (Claretians). September 9, 2021.

————. Address to the Participants in the Meeting of Moderators of Lay Associations, Ecclesial Movements, and New Communities. September 16, 2021.

————. Address to the Participants in the Third World Congress of Ecclesial Movements and New Communities. November 22, 2014.

————. *Angelus.* January 30, 2022.

————. Apostolic Constitution *Praedicate Evangelium* on the Roman Curia and Its Service to the Church in the World. March 19, 2022.

————. Apostolic Exhortation *Evangelii gaudium* on the Proclamation of the Gospel in Today's World. November 24, 2013.

————. Apostolic Letter *Desiderio desideravi* on the Liturgical Formation of the People of God. June 29, 2022.

————. Encyclical Letter *Laudato si'* on Care for our Common Home. May 24, 2015.

————. Homily of Pentecost for the Ecclesial Movements. May 19, 2013.

Fraternidade das Novas Comunidades do Brasil, ed. *Novas comunidades: Primavera da Igreja.* São Paulo: Editora Canção Nova, 2008.

Fusco, Roberto, Giancarlo Rocca, and Stefano, Vita. *La svolta dell'innovazione: Le nuove forme di vita consacrata.* Rome: Urbaniana University Press, 2015.

Ghirlanda, Gianfranco. "Charism and Juridical Status of the Ecclesial Movements." In *Movements in the Church: Proceedings of the World Congress of the Ecclesial Movements, Rome, 27–29*

May, 1998. Edited by Pontifical Council for the Laity, 128–145. Vatican City: Pontificium Consilium pro Laicis, 1999.

———. "Consilia evangelica in vita laicali." *Periodica* 87 (1998): 567–589.

———. "Nuove forme di vita consacrata in relazione al can. 605." In *Nuove forme di vita consacrata.* Edited by R. Fusco and G. Rocca, 55–71. Rome: Urbaniana University Press, 2010.

Gonzalez, Philippe and Paul Philibert. "Les communautés nouvelles: Une réception de Vatican II." *Lumen vitae* 62 (2007): 419–431.

Hanna, Tony. *New Ecclesial Movements: Communion and Liberation, Neo-Catechumenal Way, Charismatic Renewal.* Staten Island, NY: Alba House, 2006.

Hegge, Christoph. "I movimenti ecclesiali e la ricezione del Concilio Vaticano II." *Periodica de re canonica* 88 (1999): 501–532.

Illanes, José Luis. "La discusión teológica sobre la noción de laico." *Scripta theologica* 22 (1990): 771–789.

John Paul II. Apostolic Exhortation *Christifideles laici* on the Vocation and the Mission of the Lay Faithful in the Church and in the World. December 30, 1988.

———. Apostolic Exhortation *Ecclesia in America* on the Encounter with the Living Jesus Christ: The Way to Conversion, Communion, and Solidarity in America. January 22, 1999.

———. Apostolic Exhortation *Pastores dabo vobis* on the Formation of Priests in the Circumstances of the Present Day. March 25, 1992.

————. Apostolic Exhortation *Vita consecrata* on the Consecrated Life and Its Mission in the Church and in the World. March 25, 1996.

————. Apostolic Letter *Novo millenio ineunte* at the Close of the Great Jubilee of the Year 2000. January 6, 2001.

————. *The Catechism of the Catholic Church.* Vatican City: Libreria Editrice Vaticana, 1993.

————. *The Code of Canon Law.*

————. Encyclical Letter *Redemptoris missio* on the Permanent Validity of the Church's Missionary Mandate. December 7, 1990.

————. Message to the Participants in the Seminar on Ecclesial Movements and New Communities. June 18, 1999.

Kovač, Miriam. "I consacrati e i movimenti ecclesiali." *Quaderni di diritto ecclesiale* 11 (1998): 86–95.

Latin American Episcopal Conference (CELAM). *The Aparecida Document.* Bogotá: CELAM, 2007.

Leahy, Brendan. *Ecclesial Movements and Communities. Abridged 2nd ed.: Origins, Significance, and Issues.* Hyde Park, NY: New City Press, 2017.

Leidi, Leonello. "Connaître et discerner les nouvelles formes de consécration." *Vies consacrées* 87 (2015): 30–43.

LeRouzès, Dominic. "Le droit canonique et les communautés nouvelles." *Studia canonica* 40 (2006): 397–415.

Longhitano, Adolfo. "Laico, persona, fedele cristiano. Quale categoria giuridica fondamentale per i battezzati?" In *Il fedele cristiano. La condizione giuridica dei battezzati.* Edited by A. Longhitano, 9–54. Bologna: EDB, 1989.

McCord, H. Richard, "Ecclesial Movements as Agents of a New Evangelization." Resource for Catechetical Sunday. Washington, DC: USCCB, September 16, 2012. Accessed January 22nd, 2022. https://www.usccb.org/beliefs-and-teachings/how-we-teach/catechesis/catechetical-sunday/new-evangelization/upload/ecclesial-movements-mccord.pdf).

McDermott, Rose. "The Ninth Ordinary Session of the Synod of Bishops: Four Moments and Six Canonical Issues." *Commentarium pro religiosis et missionariis* 77 (1996): 261–294.

Martínez Sistach, Lluís. *Las asociaciones de fieles*. Barcelona: Aranzadi, 1986.

Martins Terra, João Evangelista. *Os novos movimentos eclesiais*. São Paulo: Editora Canção Nova, 2010.

National Conference of Bishops of Brazil (CNBB). *Community of Communities: A New Parish*. São Paulo: Editora Paulinas, 2014.

———. *A Igreja e os novos grupos religiosos*. São Paulo: Edições CNBB, 1993.

———. *Igreja particular, movimentos eclesiais e novas comunidades—Particular church, ecclesial movements and new communities*. Brasília: Edições CNBB, 2009.

———. *Lay Christians in Church and Society*. São Paulo: Edições CNBB, 2019.

———. *Mission and Ministries of Lay Christians*. Itaici: Editora Paulinas, 1999.

Navarro, Luís, "I nuovi movimenti ecclesiali nel magistero di Benedetto XVI." *Ius Ecclesiae* 21 (2009): 569–584.

———. "Lo statuto giuridico del laico: Sacerdozio comune e secolarità." *Fidelium iura* 7 (1997): 71–101.

Nogueria, Oquendo and Emir, Maria. *Nas mãos do Oleiro: Formação para as comunidades novas.* Fortaleza: Editora Shalom, 2011.

Oberti, Armando. "Les Instituts séculiers dans le nouveau code de droit canonique." *Vies consacrée* 55 (1983): 201–212.

Ouellet, Marc. *L'apport des mouvements ecclésiaux: Unité et diversité dans l'Esprit.* Bruyères-le-Châtel: Nouvelle Cité, 2011.

———. *Evangelizing by Attraction: The People of God as a People of Joy; The Permanent Fecundity of the Charisms Reveals Itself in Communion and in Mission.* Conference at the Congress of Ecclesial Movements and New Communities. Rome, November 20, 2014.

Paul VI. Apostolic Constitution *Laudis canticum* Promulgating the Divine Office as Revised in Accordance with the Decree of the Second Ecumenical Council of the Vatican. November 1, 1970.

Pius XI. Encyclical Letter *Ubi arcano Dei consilio* on the Peace of Christ in the Kingdom of Christ. December 23, 1922.

Pius XII. Apostolic Constitution *Bis saeculari die* on Marian Congregations. September 27, 1948.

———. *Potenza e influsso della Chiesa.* February 20, 1946.

———. Motu Proprio *Primo feliciter.* March 12, 1948.

———. Apostolic Constitution *Provida Mater Ecclesia* concerning Secular Institutes. February 2, 1947.

Ratzinger, Joseph. Address to the Chilean Bishops. July 13, 1988.

———. "Dialogue with Joseph Card. Ratzinger." In *The Ecclesial Movements in the Pastoral Concern of the Bishops.* Edited by

Pontifical Council for the Laity, 225–258. Vatican City: Pontificium Consilium pro Laicis, 2000.

———. "The Ecclesial Movements: A Theological Reflection on Their Place in the Church." In *Movements in the Church: Proceedings of the World Congress of the Ecclesial Movements, Rome, 27–29 May, 1998.* Edited by Pontifical Council for the Laity, 23–51. Vatican City: Pontificium Consilium pro Laicis, 1999.

———. *The Feast of Faith: Approaches to a Theology of the Liturgy.* San Francisco, CA: Ignatius Press, 1986.

———. *The Ratzinger Report: An Exclusive Interview on the State of the Church.* San Francisco, CA: Ignatius Press, 1985.

———. *The Spirit of the Liturgy.* San Francisco, CA: Ignatius Press, 2000.

Recchi, Silvia. "I movimenti ecclesiali e l'incardinazione dei sacerdoti membri." *Quaderni di diritto ecclesiale* 15 (2002): 168–176.

———. "Per una configurazione canonica dei movimenti ecclesiali." *Quaderni di diritto ecclesiale* 11 (1998): 57–66.

Rocca, Giancarlo. "Le nuove comunità." *Quaderni di diritto ecclesiale* 5 (1992): 163–176.

Roullet, Hervé. *Être laïc et se former dans l'Église d'aujourd'hui.* Bordeaux: D. F. R., 2010.

Ruini, Camillo. "Tangible Ecclesial Communion." In *Pastors and the Ecclesial Movements.* Edited by Pontifical Council for the Laity, 197–199. Vatican City: Libreria Editrice Vaticana, 2009.

Rylko, Stanislaw. "Ecclesial Movements and New Communities: The Response of the Holy Spirit to Today's Challenge of Evangelization." Address given in Bogotá. March 9, 2006.

————. "The Event of 30 May 1998 and its Ecclesiological and Pastoral Consequences for the Life of the Church." In *The Ecclesial Movements in the Pastoral Concern of the Bishops*. Edited by Pontifical Council for the Laity, 23–46. Vatican City: Pontificium Consilium pro Laicis, 2000.

Sabbarese, Luigi. "L'autorità nelle nuove comunità." In *Nuove forme di vita consacrata*. Edited by R. Fusco and G. Rocca, 91–112. Rome: Urbaniana University Press, 2010.

Schillebeeckx, Edward. "Definizione del laico cristiano." In *La Chiesa del Vaticano II*. Edited by G. Baraúna, 959–977. Florence: Vallecchi, 1965.

Second Vatican Council. *Acta Synodalia*.

————. Constitution *Sacrosanctum Concilium* on the Sacred Liturgy. December 4, 1963.

————. Decree *Apostolicam actuositatem* on the Apostolate of the Laity. November 18, 1965.

————. Decree *Optatam totius* on Priestly Training. October 28, 1965.

————. Decree *Perfectae caritatis* on the Adaptation and Renewal of Religious Life. October 28, 1965.

————. Decree *Unitatis redintegratio* on Ecumenism. November 21, 1964.

————. Dogmatic Constitution *Lumen gentium* on the Church. November 21, 1964.

————. Dogmatic Constitution *Dei Verbum* on Divine Revelation. November 18, 1965.

———. Pastoral Constitution *Gaudium et spes* on the Church in the Modern World. December 7, 1965.

Torres, Jesús. "Criteri di approvazione delle nuove comunità: La prassi della Congregazione per gli Istituti di Vita Consacrata e le Società di Vita Apostolica." In *Nuove forme di vita consacrata*. Edited by R. Fusco and G. Rocca, 219–225. Rome: Urbaniana University Press, 2010.

Timbó, Sidney. *Novas comunidades: Uma novidade no Brasil e no mundo*. Fortaleza: Editora Shalom, 2004.

United States Conference of Catholic Bishops (USCCB). *Called and Gifted for the Third Millennium*. Washington, DC: USCCB Publishing, 1995.

———. *Co-Workers in the Vineyard of the Lord: A Resource for Guiding the Development of Lay Ecclesial Ministry*. Washington, DC: USCCB Publishing, 2005.

———. *Sing to the Lord: Music in Divine Worship*. Washington, DC: USCCB Publishing, 2007.

Villemin, Laurent. "L'éclosion des nouveaux mouvements: Une question à l'ecclésiologie." *Lumen vitae* 62 (2007): 367–377.

von Balthasar, Hans Urs. "Chi è un laico?" *Communio* 83/4 (1985): 4–11.

Zadra, Barbara. "L'assunzione dei consigli evangelici negli statuti delle associazioni che prevedono la consacrazione di vita." *Quaderni di diritto ecclesiale* 12 (1999): 353–362.

Zanetti, Eugenio. "I laici." In *Fedeli, Associazioni, Movimenti*. Edited by Gruppo Italiano Docenti di Diritto Canonico, 33–63. Milan: Edizioni glossa, 2002.

About the Author

Fr. Nilson Leal de Sá is a priest of the Community of the Beatitudes, for many years serving the Church in Europe, Africa, Asia, and the Americas. With a doctorate in canon law and a master's in theology, Fr. Nilson has ministered in different areas of government, academia, and ecclesiastical and parish life.

Sophia Institute

SOPHIA INSTITUTE IS A nonprofit institution that seeks to nurture the spiritual, moral, and cultural life of souls and to spread the gospel of Christ in conformity with the authentic teachings of the Roman Catholic Church.

Sophia Institute Press fulfills this mission by offering translations, reprints, and new publications that afford readers a rich source of the enduring wisdom of mankind.

Sophia Institute also operates the popular online resource CatholicExchange.com. *Catholic Exchange* provides world news from a Catholic perspective as well as daily devotionals and articles that will help readers to grow in holiness and live a life consistent with the teachings of the Church.

In 2013, Sophia Institute launched Sophia Institute for Teachers to renew and rebuild Catholic culture through service to Catholic education. With the goal of nurturing the spiritual, moral, and cultural life of souls, and an abiding respect for the role and work of teachers, we strive to provide materials and programs that are at once enlightening to the mind and ennobling to the heart; faithful and complete, as well as useful and practical.

Sophia Institute gratefully recognizes the Solidarity Association for preserving and encouraging the growth of our apostolate over the course of many years. Without their generous and timely support, this book would not be in your hands.

www.SophiaInstitute.com
www.CatholicExchange.com
www.SophiaInstituteforTeachers.org

Sophia Institute Press is a registered trademark of Sophia Institute.
Sophia Institute is a tax-exempt institution as defined by the
Internal Revenue Code, Section 501(c)(3). Tax ID 22-2548708.